10-Minute Poetry Activities Across the Curriculum

by

Jean Pottle

J. WESTON
WALCH
PUBLISHER

Portland, Maine

User's Guide to *Walch Reproducible Books*

As part of our general effort to provide educational materials that are as practical and economical as possible, we have designated this publication a "reproducible book." The designation means that purchase of the book includes purchase of the right to limited reproduction of all pages on which this symbol appears:

Here is the basic Walch policy: We grant to individual purchasers of this book the right to make sufficient copies of reproducible pages for use by all students of a single teacher. This permission is limited to a single teacher and does not apply to entire schools or school systems, so institutions purchasing the book should pass the permission on to a single teacher. Copying of the book or its parts for resale is prohibited.

Any questions regarding this policy or requests to purchase further reproduction rights should be addressed to:

Permissions Editor
J. Weston Walch, Publisher
321 Valley Street • P.O. Box 658
Portland, Maine 04104-0658

1 2 3 4 5 6 7 8 9 10

ISBN 0-8251-4136-2

Copyright © 2000
J. Weston Walch, Publisher
P. O. Box 658 • Portland, Maine 04104-0658
www.walch.com

Printed in the United States of America

For Kemp Pottle
1930–1999

CREDITS

Page 5: Used with permission from the publisher, Alfred A. Knopf, *THE DREAM KEEPER AND OTHER POEMS,* Copyright, 1960.

Page 13: Reprinted with the permission of Simon & Schuster Books for Young Readers, an imprint of Simon & Schuster Children's Publishing Division from *Poems* by Rachel Field (Macmillan, New York, 1957)

Pages 29 and 69: Reprinted by permission of the publishers and the Trustees of Amherst College from *The Poems of Emily Dickinson,* Thomas H. Johnson, ed., Cambridge, Mass.: The Belknap Press of Harvard University Press, Copyright ©1951, 1955, 1979, 1983 by the President and Fellows of Harvard College.

Page 77: From: *Dust of Snow* from *The Poetry of Robert Frost* edited by Edward Connery Lathem. Copyright 1951 by Robert Frost. Copyright 1923, ©1969 by Henry Holt and Company, Inc. Reprinted by permission of Henry Holt and Company, Inc.

Page 89: Used by permission of Charlotte Baker Montgomery.

Page 115: Copyright ©1956 by Gwendolyn Brooks Blakely. Used by permission of HarperCollins Publishers.

Contents

Introduction . . . . *vii*

1. I Meant to Do My Work Today
   Richard Le Gallienne 1

2. Hold Fast to Dreams
   Langston Hughes 5

3. America for Me
   Henry van Dyke 9

4. Something Told the Wild Geese
   Rachel Field 13

5. Father William
   Lewis Carroll 17

6. The Dark Hills
   Edwin Arlington Robinson 21

7. How Doth the Little Crocodile
   Lewis Carroll 25

8. A Bird Came Down the Walk
   Emily Dickinson 29

9. Stars
   Sara Teasdale 33

10. Casey at the Bat
    Ernest Lawrence Thayer 37

11. The Eagle
    Alfred, Lord Tennyson 42

12. The Mountain and the Squirrel
    Ralph Waldo Emerson 46

13. Jabberwocky
    Lewis Carroll 50

14. Check
    James Stephens 53

15. Full Fathom Five
    William Shakespeare....................57

16. Ozymandias
    Percy Bysshe Shelley....................61

17. In Flanders Fields
    John McCrae....................65

18. I'm Nobody! Who Are You?
    Emily Dickinson....................69

19. The Golf Links
    Sarah N. Cleghorn....................73

20. Dust of Snow
    Robert Frost....................77

21. Overheard on a Saltmarsh
    Saki (H.H. Munro)....................81

22. The Bee
    Isaac Watts....................85

23. Days
    Karle Wilson Baker....................89

24. The Plaint of the Camel
    Charles Edward Carryl....................94

25. Our Lips and Ears
    Unknown....................98

26. Concord Hymn
    Ralph Waldo Emerson....................102

27. Thanksgiving Day
    Lydia Maria Child....................107

28. Waltzing Matilda
    A. B. Banjo Paterson....................111

29. We Real Cool
    Gwendolyn Brooks....................115

30. Eldorado
    Edgar Allan Poe....................119

INTRODUCTION

This book suggests ways you can interest your students in poetry by combining it with the study of social studies, math, science, music, art, language arts, and geography. More importantly, it helps you make poetry a permanent part of the lives of your students by asking them to memorize some or all of the poems included in this book. Of course, it is not necessary for your students to memorize the poems in order to enjoy and learn from the poems and associated activities you will find here.

If you decide to ask your students to memorize some of the selections, don't be surprised or discouraged if the idea is initially met with resistance. This will change as they gain pride in their ability to memorize and enjoy poetry.

Listed below are several reasons why memorizing poetry is a worthwhile activity.

1. Once memorized, a poem is yours forever.
2. Knowing a poem leads to understanding of that poem.
3. Poetry encourages a love of language.
4. Poetry can be shared.
5. Poetry can be an introduction to interesting people and places.
6. Poetry gives words to feelings.
7. Poetry is a link to the past as well as to the future.
8. Reciting poetry is a good way to begin or end the school day.
9. Reciting poetry builds speaking confidence.
10. Memorizing poetry can be fun!

To help students memorize the poems in this book, use the procedures outlined on the next page.

Day 1

To help students memorize the poem, first read it out loud. Then read through it again, pausing after each line and asking students to repeat the line. Work on the first stanza only.

Next, distribute copies of the poem. Team each student up with a "poetry partner." Pairs of students should then take turns repeating the first stanza. Some students will have memorized the first stanza within a few minutes.

Ask a student or two to recite the first stanza. If necessary, assign the first stanza as memorization homework.

Day 2

Ask for volunteers to recite the first stanza of the poem. Allow students to stand by their desks as they speak, rather than stand at the front of the room. This gives them an opportunity to feel more comfortable in delivering their oral presentation. Next, have students recite the poem to their poetry partners (set up on Day 1). The entire lesson can be completed in fewer than ten minutes.

Day 3

Introduce the second stanza, following the procedure outlined above. By Day 5, students should feel comfortable reciting the poem to their poetry partners or to the entire class.

I Meant to Do My Work Today

I meant to do my work today—
But a brown bird sang in the apple-tree,
And a butterfly flitted across the field,
And all the leaves were calling me.

And the wind went sighing over the land,
Tossing the grasses to and fro,
And a rainbow held out its shining hand—
So what could I do but laugh and go?

—*Richard Le Gallienne*

TEACHER PAGE

I Meant to Do My Work Today

Procedure

Use the approach to memorization outlined in the Introduction. At the same time, encourage students to discuss the content of the poem. What is the author saying? Have students ever had a similar experience? What kind of things "call" to them?

The activity sheets that accompany this poem are designed to help students make connections between the poem and nature. Encourage students to investigate "brown birds" and butterflies to deepen their understanding of the poem.

Interdisciplinary Activities

1. **Place of birth** The poet Richard Le Gallienne was born in Liverpool, England, in 1866. Your students might be interested to know that this is also the birthplace of the Beatles, who caused such a stir in the music world in the 1960s. If possible, play a Beatles recording, pointing out that song lyrics can often be read as poetry. (Language Arts, Social Studies, Music)

2. **Literary map and time line** Le Gallienne spent 30 years of his life in the United States. He was born in England during the reign of Queen Victoria, and he died in America during the presidency of Harry S Truman in 1947. Students can begin a poetry time line with Le Gallienne's birth year. (Language Arts, Social Studies)

3. **Rhyme scheme** Teach the rhyme scheme of the poem by asking students to assign a different letter of the alphabet to each line of the poem with a different ending rhyme. Lines with similar ending rhymes should be assigned the same alphabet letter. Point out that this poem is divided into two groups of lines, each of which is called a *stanza*. The rhyme scheme for the first stanza is *a-b-c-b*. Stanza 2 has a rhyme scheme of d-e-d-e. (Language Arts)

4. **Visit to elderly** Residents of elderly housing complexes enjoy seeing and hearing children. Perhaps you can arrange a visit to such a facility, and as part of your visit your students can recite this poem. The residents may surprise you by responding with poems of their own. (Language Arts, Social Studies)

5. **Personification** Teach *personification* by asking students which lines in the poem give human qualities to forces of nature. They should be able to recognize "the wind went sighing over the land" and "a rainbow held out its shining hand." (Language Arts)

6. **Etymology** To help students develop an appreciation for words, ask how they think the word *rainbow* originated. Elicit from them the observation that this natural phenomenon appears after or during a rain shower and is shaped like a bow. This would also be a good time to investigate why rainbows form. (Language Arts, Science)

Answers

Activity Sheet B

All names listed refer to butterflies.

Activity Sheet A

STUDENT PAGE

Name _____ Date _____

I Meant to Do My Work Today

Use a field guide to determine which of the following "brown birds" sing in your area. After the name of each bird, indicate the bird's range—that is, where the bird can be found. Some birds' ranges might be limited to one state. Others may be found in several states. Begin by writing the name of the field guide you are using on the line indicated. Be sure to write the page number on which you found the information for each bird.

FIELD GUIDE _____

House sparrow (page   ) _____

Cowbird (page   ) _____

Brown thrasher (page   ) _____

Longspur (page   ) _____

Winter wren (page   ) _____

Carolina wren (page   ) _____

House wren (page   ) _____

Thrush (page   ) _____

Activity Sheet B STUDENT PAGE

Name _____ Date _____

I Meant to Do My Work Today

Butterflies are among the world's most beautiful insects. They are also creatures with some of the most fanciful names. Which of the following names belong to butterflies? Circle them.

hercules	pirate
tiger	water
black oyster catcher	owl
goliath	emperor
admiral	skipper lady
harlequin	

Select one name that particularly appeals to you. Draw a picture of this butterfly below. You can use a field guide for reference.

© 2000 J. Weston Walch, Publisher

Hold Fast to Dreams

Hold fast to dreams

For if dreams die

Life is a broken-winged bird

That cannot fly.

Hold fast to dreams

For when dreams go

Life is a barren field

Frozen with snow.

—*Langston Hughes*

Hold Fast to Dreams

Procedure

Dreams are important no matter what our age. Students need to know that dreams frequently inspire people to strive for happiness in spite of adversity. Hughes encourages all of us to dream.

Follow the procedure for memorizing poems outlined in the Introduction.

Activity Sheet A leads students to create their own dream poem. Activity Sheet B connects the poem with Martin Luther King, Jr.'s "I Have a Dream" speech, and asks students to describe their own "American dream."

Interdisciplinary Activities

1. **Literary map and time line** Langston Hughes was born in Joplin, Missouri, on February 1, 1902. Ask students to find Joplin on a map of the United States. Hughes's father emigrated to Mexico in an attempt to establish a law practice. Hughes moved from place to place with his mother, joining his father in Mexico for a short time. From there, he moved to Kansas and later to Cleveland, Ohio. In 1921, Hughes entered Columbia University in New York City. School was of little interest, and when he was 21 he sailed to West Africa. Later he lived in Washington, D.C., before moving back to New York where he lived in Harlem. It was there during the Great Depression of the 1930s that Hughes saw the struggle of ordinary people during a time of great trouble in the United States. He died in 1967. Distribute maps of the United States and ask students to locate the various places Hughes called home. Make the mapping of a poet's homes an ongoing activity to which students will add the homes of other poets. (Social Studies, Language Arts, Geography)

2. **African-American rights** Discuss the problems African Americans faced during that time period and the impact they might have had on the poem. Hughes' parents were a good example of people who tried desperately to get ahead but found it impossible. Ask students why they had to leave the United States in order for Hughes' father to follow the legal profession. (Social Studies)

3. **Rhyme scheme** Ask students to identify the rhyme scheme. In each stanza, the second and fourth lines rhyme, making the rhyme scheme *a-b-c-b*. (Language Arts)

4. **Historical events** Ask for volunteers to prepare reports on historical events that affected Hughes' life. Possibilities are the Great Depression, Harlem Renaissance, and the Civil Rights Movement. (Social Studies, Language Arts)

5. **Context and word meaning** Discuss how the context of a word can alter the meaning. Use "fast" from the first line of this poem as an example. Most students will think it means "quick" or "to refrain from eating." Ask them if that makes sense in the context of the poem and what else it might mean. Perhaps they can think of other words that have more than one meaning, such as run, cuff, box, and sign. (Language Arts)

Activity Sheet A

STUDENT PAGE

Name _____ Date _____

Hold Fast to Dreams

What are your dreams? Fill in the blanks to create your own dream poem.

MY DREAM

In December I dream of _____.

January's dreams are of _____.

February brings me dreams of _____.

March's dreams are of _____.

In April my sleep brings me dreams of _____.

May and June promise dreams of _____.

Through the summer months my dreams are of _____

and _____.

With September, October, November, come dreams of _____ ,

and then it's December again.

Activity Sheet B STUDENT PAGE

Name _____ Date _____

Hold Fast to Dreams

Martin Luther King, Jr., was a man with a dream. He dreamed of a time when all people would be equal. King, who was born in 1929 in Atlanta, Georgia, lived at a time when equality was stated in the Constitution, but was not part of daily life for African Americans. King based much of his thinking on the principles of Mohandas K. Gandhi, the Indian philosopher, teacher, and nationalist leader. Gandhi preached a nonviolent approach to the social problems of his country. Following Gandhi's nonviolent methods, King helped organize the Civil Rights movement that rocked the United States in the 1950s and 1960s.

His "I Have a Dream!" speech, given in Washington, D.C., on August 28, 1963, shows the passion King felt for civil rights. A famous excerpt from this speech is, "I say to you today, my friends, that even though we face the difficulties of today and tomorrow, I still have a dream. It is a dream deeply rooted in the American dream."

Think about this excerpt. Then write a paragraph in which you describe *your* idea of the American dream. If you're familiar with all of the speech, you may begin your paragraph by explaining what you think Martin Luther King meant by his American dream. If you have time, you might want to use the Internet to learn more about Martin Luther King before you start to write.

America for Me

'Tis fine to see the Old World, and travel up and down
Among the famous palaces and cities of renown,
To admire the crumbly castles and the statues of the kings,—
But now I think I've had enough of antiquated things.

So it's home again, and home again, America for me!
My heart is turning home again, and there I long to be
In the land of youth and freedom beyond the open bars,
Where the air is full of sunlight and the flag is full of stars.

—*Henry van Dyke*

TEACHER PAGE

America for Me

Procedure

The student page includes the first two stanzas of "America for Me," a six-stanza poem. The first two stanzas set the mood of the poem and give students an opportunity to think about what is meant by the "New World." This poem can also lead to discussions about the opportunities that America has traditionally offered to its citizens and to people who immigrate to this country.

Follow the procedure described in the Introduction for helping students memorize poetry.

To help students understand this poem, discuss the following:

1. For many people who came to America from Europe, Europe was the Old World, the world they were leaving behind. America was the New World, where they hoped to make new lives for themselves.
2. Renown—fame, celebrity
3. Antiquated—aged, very old; also, old-fashioned, obsolete

Activity Sheet A gives students an outline for interviewing someone who came to America from another country. Activity Sheet B guides students through finding out information about their families as they create a "family flag."

Interdisciplinary Activities

1. **New World, Old World** Ask students to compare and contrast the New World with the Old by listing what van Dyke found in each. The Old World has palaces, famous cities, crumbly castles, and statues of kings. Students should note that the poet does not describe anything that seems fresh and open. The New World, on the other hand, has youth, freedom, sunlight, and a flag full of stars. This discussion might lead to a consideration of why America is called the "land of opportunity." Why did so many people leave the Old World to settle here? This would also pose an opportunity to discuss today's immigrants. If you have a diverse student population, expand this lesson to encompass the areas from which your students or their families have emigrated. (Social Studies, Language Arts)

2. **Immigrant interview** Have students interview someone who has moved to America from another country. (An interview sheet follows.) During a follow-up class, students should compare their answers. Ask them to label the countries they heard about on a map. (Social Studies, Language Arts)

3. **Patriotic songs** Many students today do not have any knowledge of the songs that have traditionally been sung in praise of this country. Ask if they know "God Bless America," "America the Beautiful," and the national anthem, "The Star-Spangled Banner." Then hand out the lyrics to these songs. Open a discussion about the relationship between song lyrics and poetry. If possible, team up with the music teacher and arrange to have your students listen to and discuss the words of these famous songs. (Social Studies, Language Arts, Music)

4. **Literary map and time line** Henry van Dyke was born in Germantown, Pennsylvania, in 1852 and died in 1933. Add his birthdate to your class time line and mark Germantown as his birthplace on your classroom literary map. Also map Princeton, where van Dyke attended the university and spent much of his professional life as a pastor. (Social Studies, Language Arts)

5. **Pledge of Allegiance** Ask students to write the "Pledge of Allegiance" from memory. Copy the "Pledge" on a transparency and let students compare their versions to the original. Discuss any variations between the actual words and students' versions. (Language Arts, Social Studies)

Activity Sheet A   **STUDENT PAGE**

Name _____ Date _____

America for Me: Interview Sheet

Talk with a friend, neighbor, or relative who was born in another country. By asking the questions that follow, you will discover why people leave their homelands to settle in the United States.

1. In what country were you born? _____

2. When did you move to this country? _____

3. How is America different from your homeland? _____
   _____

4. What do you miss most about your homeland? _____
   _____

5. What do you like most about America? _____
   _____

6. Do you remember a song or poem about your country? Would you recite it for me? (If possible, tape the material. Otherwise, write out the words of the song or poem on the back of this sheet.) _____
   _____

7. May I read you a poem? Please give me your reaction to the poet's words. (Recite "America for Me." Write the person's reaction here.)
   _____
   _____

Activity Sheet B　　　　　　　　　　　　　　　　　　　　**STUDENT PAGE**

Name _____ Date _____

America for Me: Creating a Family Flag

If countries and states can have flags, why can't your family? Use the questions below to collect information about your family. Write your responses on the back of this sheet, or on a separate piece of paper. Then, design a flag for your family. A plain sheet of paper will be just fine. You may want to color the background of your flag, and then add symbols and names in appropriate places. This part is up to you: be creative! Finish by writing the family motto in bold letters at the bottom of the page.

1. List the names of your family members.

2. List the various activities your family members enjoy. Are there some that you enjoy doing together?

3. From what country or countries did your family originate? Look up those countries' flags on the Internet or in a reference book. Note the colors of the flag on your work page. If you don't know the specific country, pick two or three colors that you particularly like.

4. Decide on a symbol to represent the various activities you listed above. For example, if sports are of interest, you might use a football, basketball, or baseball bat to represent this interest. A book would be a good symbol for families that enjoy reading, or a television screen for those that like to watch TV. Draw these symbols on your work page. Remember, your artwork doesn't have to be fancy.

5. What is a favorite family expression? Maybe it's as simple as, "Let's have popcorn," or, "We want pizza." Choose an expression that you think could be your family's motto.

© 2000 J. Weston Walch, Publisher　　　　　　12　　　　　10-Minute Poetry Activities Across the Curriculum

Something Told the Wild Geese

Something told the wild geese
    It was time to go.
Though the fields lay golden
    Something whispered—"Snow."
Leaves were green and stirring,
    Berries, luster-glossed,
But beneath warm feathers
    Something cautioned—"Frost."
All the sagging orchards
    Steamed with amber spice,
But each wild breast stiffened
    At remembered ice.
Something told the wild geese
    It was time to fly—
Summer sun was on their wings,
    Winter in their cry.

—Rachel Field

TEACHER PAGE

Something Told the Wild Geese

Procedure

Follow the procedure for memorizing outlined in the Introduction. Students will find the first stanza particularly easy to memorize because of the repetition of the word "something." If you live in a part of the world where Canada geese are seen and heard as the seasons change, students will easily relate to this poem.

Activity Sheet A presents an activity you can use to introduce students to the topic of migration. Activity Sheet B is a scrambled word puzzle that introduces some words students may encounter as they read about migration.

Interdisciplinary Activities

1. **Literary map and time line** Rachel Field was born in New York City in 1894 and died in 1942. Mention to your class that two world wars were fought during her lifetime. She did not live to see the end of World War II. She received the Newbery Medal for children's literature in 1929 for *Hitty,* the story of a doll. Have students add Field to the literary time line and map. (Geography)

2. **Bird calls** If possible, play the call of the Canada goose for your students. "Birding by Ear," a Peterson Field Guide by Richard K. Walton and Robert W. Lawson, contains the call of the Canada goose, as well as many other bird calls. Cornell Laboratory of Ornithology has a web site at http://birdsource.cornell.edu where you can hear recordings of bird songs. (Language Arts)

3. **Migration** Use this poem to introduce the study of migration. As a first step, discuss general reasons for the migration of birds and people. Get students to notice that in the first stanza the birds recognize that change is in the air. Ask if this is also true for people. Why do people move from one place to another? "Better opportunities" and "better weather" will probably be among the answers. Just like migrating birds, people sometimes have to move to new locations in order to survive. Point out that people rely on their ability to think. What do birds rely on? Students will most likely answer "instinct." Continue by asking what other birds migrate from winter to summer habitats. Distribute copies of activity sheet A, "Birds on the Move." Ask each student to research a specific bird from among those listed on the activity sheet. (Language Arts, Science, Geography)

4. **Migration map** As a follow-up to this assignment, ask students to trace the migration route of the birds they have chosen from winter to summer homes. If possible, use a large classroom map to have students fill in the routes their birds follow. (Geography, Science)

5. **Wacky birds** Encourage students to have fun with bird names. Using the names listed on Activity Sheet A, have students compile a bird dictionary. The definitions should be determined by the names alone. For example, a cowbird could be an unusual bird that can be milked. Set up a committee to review the definitions and organize them into a booklet. Students who enjoy drawing and painting can illustrate the final draft of the dictionary, which can then be shared with other classes or placed in the school library. (Art, Language Arts)

Answers

Activity Sheet B

1. habitat
2. migration
3. robin
4. nest
5. flight
6. animal
7. oriole
8. meadowlark
9. beak
10. soar
11. crow

Activity Sheet A

STUDENT PAGE

Name _____ Date _____

Something Told the Wild Geese: Birds on the Move

From the list of birds below, select one that you think might be of interest to you. Using the Internet and field guides, research the questions below. Write your answers on a separate sheet of paper or on the back of this one. Then think of an interesting and original way to present this material to your class. One possibility is to write a "bird talk" column for a classroom newspaper.

American crow	oriole
blue jay	hummingbird
song sparrow	Carolina wren
grosbeak	snipe
eastern bluebird	meadowlark
robin	pelican
mallard	cowbird
mockingbird	catbird

1. What is the winter home of your bird?
2. What is the spring and summer home of your bird?
3. What does your bird eat?
4. Why does (or doesn't) your bird migrate?
5. How far does your bird travel between its summer and winter habitats?
6. What are some of the other birds in this bird's family?

Activity Sheet B   **STUDENT PAGE**

Name _____ Date _____

Something Told the Wild Geese

This word scramble contains eleven bird-related words. Can you find them and list them on the lines below? Approximate how long you think this will take. Write that number here _____

Now begin, being sure to record your starting and ending times to see how close you come to your projected time.

Starting Time: _____

Ending Time: _____

1. TIABTAH _____
2. OMGNIARIT _____
3. BRNIO _____
4. TNES _____
5. IFHLTG _____
6. LAMNIA _____
7. OOLERI _____
8. WKMLRDEAOA _____
9. KBAE _____
10. RSAO _____
11. OCWR _____

© 2000 J. Weston Walch, Publisher   16   10-Minute Poetry Activities Across the Curriculum

Father William

"You are old, Father William," the young man said
  "And your hair has become very white;
And yet you incessantly stand on your head—
  Do you think, at your age, it is right?"

"In my youth," Father William replied to his son,
  "I feared it might injure the brain;
But now that I'm perfectly sure I have none,
  Why, I do it again and again."

"You are old," said the youth, "as I mentioned before,
  And have grown most uncommonly fat;
Yet you turned a back-somersault in at the door—
  Pray, what is the reason of that?"

"In my youth," said the sage, as he shook his gray locks,
  "I kept all my limbs very supple
By the use of this ointment—one shilling the box—
  Allow me to sell you a couple."

"You are old," said the youth, "and your jaws are too weak
  For anything tougher than suet;
Yet you finished the goose, with the bones and the beak—
  Pray, how did you manage to do it?"

"In my youth," said his father, "I took to the law,
  And argued each case with my wife;
And the muscular strength, which it gave to my jaw,
  Has lasted the rest of my life."

"You are old," said the youth, "one would hardly suppose
  That your eye was as steady as ever;
Yet you balanced an eel on the end of your nose—
  What made you so awfully clever?"

"I have answered three questions, and that is enough,"
  Said his father; "Don't give yourself airs!
Do you think I can listen all day to such stuff?
  Be off, or I'll kick you downstairs!"

—Lewis Carroll

TEACHER PAGE

Father William

Procedure

Lewis Carroll is the pseudonym of Charles Lutwidge Dodgson. He was born in England in 1832 and died in 1898. Best known as the author of *Alice's Adventures in Wonderland*, Carroll was educated at Rugby and Oxford and spent his professional life teaching mathematics at Oxford. He is known for his playfulness with language, as can be seen in "Father William" as well as "The Hunting of the Snark," "The Walrus and the Carpenter," and "Jabberwocky" (see page 50).

Although this is a rather long poem, most students will enjoy and easily memorize the first stanza. You will find that many wish to learn far more. The last stanza is always a favorite.

Activity Sheet A helps students to write their own poems, using "Father William" as a guide. In Activity Sheet B, students see that they can learn about things like punctuation from other writing.

Interdisciplinary Activities

1. **Old vs. young** Although the poem is written to entertain, Carroll's point is well taken: Too often young people judge older people based on little more than their age. Of course, this is also true of older people judging those who are younger. This poem offers an opportunity for students to look at the accomplishments of older people. One way to begin is to find out more about those who serve within the community as school- and hospital-board members, scout leaders, religious leaders, etc. A little research on your part will help students see the contributions made by the older generation. (Social Studies, Language Arts)

2. **Oral history** Invite older members of your community to spend time in your classroom discussing their histories and current activities. To make this a special event, serve simple refreshments. This will give you an opportunity to discuss the proper behavior for entertaining guests in the classroom. In addition, the class should follow up with thank-you notes, which will give students an opportunity to write for a specific purpose. (Social Studies, Language Arts, Etiquette)

3. **Mortality rates** Start a discussion about what age is "old." Remind students that this poem was written in the nineteenth century, when the average life span was far shorter. Have students work in groups to research the mortality rates of various periods, beginning with 50 B.C. They can then compare the mortality rates with those of today. Plot a graph to show the changes. Encourage or assign individual students to investigate the projected life spans of people in the twenty-first century. (Language Arts, Math, Social Studies)

4. **Choral reading** Divide the class in half, assigning the son's stanzas to one section and the father's to another. Have students act out the poem, with, for example, the "fathers" affecting an "older" voice and mannerisms and the "sons" those of a child. Alternately, assign individuals to read the words inside the quotation marks and others to read those outside of the quotation marks. (Language Arts)

5. **The poet's life** Ask students to research Dodgson's life using the Internet and reference books. Pose a question about the relationship between poetry and mathematics. Encourage your students to think about this as they learn about Dodgson's life. What might have attracted him to these different disciplines? (Language Arts, Mathematics, Technology)

Answers

Activity Sheet B
1. inside
2. when the question is part of the material being quoted, not the material surrounding the quote
3. inside
4. quotation marks
5. semicolon

Activity Sheet A

STUDENT PAGE

Name _____ Date _____

Father William

Write your own poem, using "Father William" as a model. Begin by thinking of an introductory quotation, for example:

"You are young, brother Jonah (Jim, Jack, or whatever name you want)."

"It is late, Aunt Teresa (Addie, Jennifer, Sasha, etc.)."

"I am hungry, Mother dear."

"It is early, Friend Ike."

Just as in "Father William," your second line should be a comment about your first statement. Make the third line of your poem rhyme with the first and the last line with the second.

Once you begin, you will find that writing a poem can be fun. Write at least two stanzas.

ROUGH DRAFT OF POEM

_____

_____

_____

_____

_____

_____

_____

Reread your poem and make any needed changes. Check your punctuation carefully and compare it to that of "Father William." Prepare a final draft and illustrate your poem.

Activity Sheet B

STUDENT PAGE

Name _____ Date _____

Father William

You can learn a great deal about correct punctuation by carefully examining the work of others. Answer the punctuation questions that follow by referring to "Father William." Write your answers on a separate sheet of paper.

1. Are commas placed inside or outside quotation marks? Write an example from the poem.

2. When are question marks placed inside quotation marks? Write an example from the poem.

3. Do periods appear inside or outside quotation marks? Write an example from the poem.

4. What punctuation marks are used to show that a specific person is speaking? Write an example from the poem.

5. What punctuation mark is used after the second line of most stanzas in this poem?

6. To show what you have learned about punctuation from reading "Father William," write your own sentences that place commas correctly in relationship to quotation marks. Do the same for periods and question marks.

The Dark Hills

Dark hills at evening in the west,

Where sunset hovers like a sound

Of golden horns that sang to rest

Old bones of warriors under ground,

Far now from all the bannered ways

Where flash the legions of the sun,

You fade—as if the last of days

Were fading, and all wars were done.

—*Edwin Arlington Robinson*

TEACHER PAGE

The Dark Hills

Procedure

This poem is easily memorized because of its straightforward rhyme scheme. Ask students to plot the *a-b-a-b-c-d-c-d* rhyme scheme. Use the memorization plan outlined in the first lesson to aid your students in memorizing this poem.

Activity Sheet A guides students through an interview with a veteran. Activity Sheet B helps students learn more about the period in which Robinson lived by examining the work of his contemporary, Winslow Homer.

Like many others, this poem can be interpreted in more than one way. Some readers see "The Dark Hills" as a poem about war, others as a metaphor for the passing ("fading") of life. If you think your students are ready to approach a poem on more than one level, have them find images in the poem that support the idea that the poem is about the end of life. Among the possibilities are "sunset hovers," "sang to rest," "You fade," and "the last of days."

Interdisciplinary Activities

1. **Literary map and time line** Edwin Arlington Robinson was born in Head Tide, Maine, in 1869. Longing for a baby girl, his parents had neglected to choose a name for a boy. He went without a name until he was six months old. Then a group of friends got together, placed names in a hat, and pulled out "Edwin." The man who had contributed "Edwin" was from Arlington, Massachusetts. Add Robinson to your class time line and literary map. (Language Arts, Social Studies)

2. **Identifying tone** Ask students to describe the tone of this poem and to support their ideas with quotations. Most will focus upon its qualities of sadness, regret, maybe despair.

   Ask students to determine Robinson's attitude toward war. Discuss his pessimism about the decline of warfare until the world ends. Connect this attitude to his birth after the Civil War, and the fact that he lived through World War I. (Social Studies, Language Arts)

3. **Poetic imagery** Ask students to illustrate the poem with the images Robinson has used ("Dark hills," "golden horns," "old bones," "flash the legions of the sun"). They might rewrite the poem, replacing its poetic imagery with pictures. (Language Arts, Art)

4. **Memorial Day** Memorial Day, originally named "Decoration Day," commemorates those who gave their lives for the United States. This poem offers an opportunity to consider the importance of Memorial Day and how it should be celebrated. Discuss with students their feelings about such a day. If you wish to carry this further, ask students to interview war veterans. If students *do* carry out this assignment, make them aware that some veterans may have disturbing memories they do not want to relive. Students should be prepared for the strong emotions that interviews may elicit. If possible, arrange the interview sheets into a booklet, which can be made available to other classes studying wars. (Language Arts, Social Studies)

5. **Theodore Roosevelt and E.A. Robinson** One of Roosevelt's sons introduced him to Robinson's poetry. Interestingly, this son was introduced to Robinson's poetry by a teacher. (Remember this on days you think teachers don't make a difference.) Roosevelt wrote Robinson a letter of appreciation for "The Children of the Night" and encouraged his own publisher to bring out some of Robinson's work. Later, Roosevelt appointed Robinson to a job at the custom house in New York City.

   Students might like to learn more about Teddy Roosevelt and his connection with Robinson. Much of this information is found in *The Oxford Book of Literary Anecdotes,* (Donald Hall, ed. New York: Oxford University Press, 1981). (Language Arts, Social Studies)

Activity Sheet A

STUDENT PAGE

Name _____ Date _____

The Dark Hills: Remembering

Interview at least two veterans who have served in the armed forces. Parents, teachers, librarians, and your local American Legion will be able to help you locate veterans who are willing to be interviewed. Explain that your interest in their experience was prompted by a discussion of the importance of Memorial Day.

1. In what branch of the armed forces did you serve? _____
   _____

2. When did you serve? Did you fight in a war? _____
   _____

3. Where were you stationed? _____
   _____

4. How old were you at the time? _____

5. What do you remember most vividly about your experiences? _____
   _____
   _____

6. How was Memorial Day celebrated when you completed your military service?
   _____

7. What changes in Memorial Day celebrations have taken place since then? How do you feel about these changes? _____
   _____
   _____
   _____

© 2000 J. Weston Walch, Publisher   10-Minute Poetry Activities Across the Curriculum

Activity Sheet B   STUDENT PAGE

Name _____ Date _____

The Dark Hills

To learn more about the world in which E. A. Robinson lived, study the work of another famous artist from this time period, the painter Winslow Homer. Homer was born in 1836 in Boston, Massachusetts. He began his career as an illustrator for *Harper's Weekly,* a popular magazine of the day. When the Civil War broke out, Homer spent time on the battlefields. He produced a series of war paintings and illustrations.

Homer also painted in France, in the Adirondack Mountains of New York State, and on the coasts of Maine and Massachusetts. His pictures hang in museums around the world. Copies of his pictures can be found on the Internet, in encyclopedias, and in other research and art books. Find a reproduction of one of Homer's pictures. Study the picture carefully. Then respond to the following questions.

1. What is the name of the painting you found? _____

2. Why do you think Homer gave it this title? _____
   _____

3. Where do you think this painting is set (France, New York State, Maine, or Massachusetts)? What evidence suggests this? _____
   _____
   _____
   _____

4. What aspects of the painting differ from contemporary life? Consider the setting, the clothing people wear, and the activities in which they are engaged.
   _____
   _____
   _____

5. What is the time period depicted in this picture? _____

© 2000 J. Weston Walch, Publisher   24   10-Minute Poetry Activities Across the Curriculum

How Doth the Little Crocodile

How doth the little crocodile
   Improve his shining tail,
And pour the waters of the Nile
   On every golden scale!

How cheerfully he seems to grin,
   How neatly spreads his claws,
And welcomes little fishes in
   With gently smiling jaws.

—Lewis Carroll

> **TEACHER PAGE**

How Doth the Little Crocodile

Procedure

This is an easy poem to remember because of its rhyme scheme: *a-b-a-b*. If students have already learned "Father William," they will look upon Lewis Carroll as an old friend. If your class has not already done so, add Carroll's dates to the class time line and map.

Activity Sheet A provides a writing frame students can use to describe an imaginary encounter with a crocodile. Activity Sheet B presents some interesting facts about crocodiles and directs students to add more information to the list.

Interdisciplinary Activities

1. **Choice of words** In this poem, Lewis Carroll lulls the reader into a false sense of security by using such words as "shining tail," "golden scale," and "grin." He gives no indication that this "little" poem is going to end in disaster for "little fishes." Ask students to discuss the poet's choice of word, in particular, the words "gently smiling jaws." Compare the expression "crocodile tears," with its implication of insincerity. Discuss the speaker's, readers', and crocodile's own views of his meal. (Language Arts)

2. **Crocodile facts** Have students check the reliability of Carroll's information on crocodiles, including such questions as whether there are golden crocodiles in the Nile and what these crocodiles eat. Students will be interested to discover that crocodiles live to be very old; in fact, one reportedly lived to be approximately 115 years old in a Russian zoo. Crocodiles are known for their speed, which can reach upwards of 30 miles an hour. They also have three different gaits, one of which resembles the manner in which dogs run. (Science, Language Arts, Research)

3. **Reptiles** Review the definition of a reptile, using the crocodile as an example. (Science)

4. **Alligators vs. crocodiles** Many people frequently confuse alligators and crocodiles. Ask students to research the similarities and differences between these two reptiles on the Internet. Encourage students to refer to a field guide on reptiles. (Science, Technology)

5. **Illustrating Lewis Carroll** Lewis Carroll wrote a number of poems featuring unlikely animals as characters. Among those your students might enjoy are "The Hunting of the Snark," "The Walrus and the Carpenter," "The Lobster Quadrille," and "The Melancholy Pig."

After reading a variety of Carroll's poems, ask students to copy and illustrate a book of his poetry. (Language Arts, Art)

Activity Sheet A   STUDENT PAGE

Name _____ Date _____

How Doth the Little Crocodile

   Crocodiles are feared by many people. Why? What is there about animals like this that we humans find so frightening? On this activity page, write a letter to a friend describing your adventure with a crocodile. You may want to do a little research first, or you can just imagine the adventure. A writing frame is provided to get you started. Do not feel restricted by the frame; use what you like and discard the rest. When you have finished, add a title.

TITLE _____

   My adventure began in _____ about _____ ago. I had been traveling through _____ when I suddenly heard _____ in the water near the path I was following. Immediately sensing _____, I moved away from _____ and looked _____ at _____.

   Whatever it was, it was big. I would say it was about _____ feet long. The color is hard to describe but let's say it looked like _____. My friends had warned me that _____ _____, so I was _____. I decided to investigate further by _____. Picking up a _____, I slowly approached the_____. As I looked down I saw _____. Suddenly I realized that _____. It didn't take me much time to _____. Whenever I tell anyone about _____, they always say, "_____."

© 2000 J. Weston Walch, Publisher   27   10-Minute Poetry Activities Across the Curriculum

Activity Sheet B   **STUDENT PAGE**

Name _____ Date _____

How Doth the Little Crocodile: Fascinating Facts About Crocodiles

The following list has some interesting information about the crocodile. How many fascinating facts can you add to this list? Use the Internet and other research sources to find information.

1. Crocodiles have pointed snouts.
2. Crocodiles are reptiles, just like snakes.
3. Saltwater crocodiles can be as long as 19 feet.
4. A female crocodile can lay as many as 40 eggs at a time.
5. Mother crocodiles carry their young from land to water in their mouths.
6. Some of the crocodile's lower teeth show, even when its mouth is closed.
7. A crocodile's body is covered with large scales.
8. Crocodiles propel themselves through the water with their tails.
9. Crocodiles can remain submerged for up to two hours.
10. Crocodiles can have as many as 3,000 teeth during their lifetimes.
11. South Florida is the only place in the world where alligators and crocodiles can be found together.
12. A crocodile cannot chew its food.

Now it's your turn. What fascinating facts can you add to this list? Write your facts on the back of this sheet or on a separate piece of paper.

© 2000 J. Weston Walch, Publisher   28   10-Minute Poetry Activities Across the Curriculum

A Bird Came Down the Walk...

A bird came down the walk —

He did not know I saw —

He bit an angleworm in halves

And ate the fellow, raw,

And then he drank a Dew

From a convenient Grass —

And then hopped sidewise to the Wall

To let a Beetle pass—

—*Emily Dickinson*

Teacher Page

A Bird Came Down the Walk...

Procedure

Only two stanzas of this five-stanza poem are included on the student page. Students who haven't had an opportunity to hear reader-friendly poems by Emily Dickinson may be surprised to learn that she wrote this poem. Don't tell your students who the author is until you have read the poem to them a couple of times; then, ask them to hypothesize about the poet. Discuss poets they know who have been interested in nature, as well as those who use everyday language. Find out when they think the poem was written.

After these questions have been broached, tell them that Emily Dickinson was born in Amherst, Massachusetts, in 1830. She is known for her love of nature and her home. At the age of 23 she wrote to a friend, "I do not go from home." She didn't—except, perhaps, in her poetry.

Activity Sheet A has students write a worm's-eye account of the events desribed in the first stanza. Activity Sheet B directs students to design a quilt block that reflects Emily Dickinson's garden.

Interdisciplinary Activities

1. **Identifying birds** Ask your students what kind of bird would bite an angleworm in half but move aside for a beetle. A little research in a field guide might suggest a variety of answers. "Hopped" and "angleworm" may suggest that the poet is describing a robin. Robins are not known to eat beetles. (Language Arts, Science)

2. **Emily Dickinson's birthday** As mentioned above, Emily Dickinson was a recluse after the age of 23. Even though she stayed at home, she was interested in the outside world. According to one anecdote, she showed her love of children by baking treats and then lowering them to children below her window in a basket. One of her favorite recipes was for gingerbread. Celebrate her birthday on December 10 by baking gingerbread and singing "Happy Birthday" to the poet. (Language Arts, Consumer Science, Music)

Activity Sheet A

STUDENT PAGE

Name _____ Date _____

A Bird Came Down the Walk . . .

This poem is written from the poet's point of view. Suppose you were in Emily Dickinson's garden the day she saw the death of the worm. Pretend you are a member of that worm's family. How would you report this crime to the other members of your family?

Before you begin writing, notice the details mentioned in the poem. Take into account that the bird is on a path of some type, that the observer does nothing to help the worm, and that the hungry robin gobbles down the halved worm. Go on to write the description of the foul act that you would pass along to the departed worm's family.

**A BIRD CAME DOWN THE WALK . . .
BY A. WORM**

_____

_____

_____

_____

_____

_____

_____

© 2000 J. Weston Walch, Publisher   10-Minute Poetry Activities Across the Curriculum

Activity Sheet B **STUDENT PAGE**

Name _____ Date _____

A Bird Came Down the Walk . . . Making a Quilt Block

One of the activities at which women of Dickinson's time worked was quilt-making. They made quilts for every occasion: a new baby, a wedding, the weather. What kind of a quilt might Dickinson have made? From her poetry, we know she appreciated nature, so perhaps her quilt would have reflected that interest.

Create a quilt pattern for Emily Dickinson. Follow the directions below to create your version of this pattern. Your classmates will do the same, so you can create an interesting display with your different interpretations.

1. On a sheet of white paper, draw nine 2- x 2-inch blocks. The blocks should form a square, three blocks wide and three blocks high.

2. On each block draw a flower, bird, tree, or anything else you think might have been in Emily's garden.

3. Add color to your quilt blocks.

Stars

Alone in the night
   On a dark hill
With pines around me
   Spicy and still,

And a heaven full of stars
   Over my head,
White and topaz
   And misty red;

Myriads with beating
   Hearts of fire
That aeons
   Cannot vex or tire;

Up the dome of heaven
   Like a great hill,
I watch them marching
   Stately and still,

And I know that I
   Am honored to be
Witness
   Of so much majesty.

—Sara Teasdale

Teacher Page

Stars

Procedure

After you have read the poem out loud a couple of times, ask if anyone in the classroom has had a similar experience. Discuss the images Sara Teasdale creates. Get students to notice that she uses visual images, as well as those that appeal to the sense of smell.

Activity Sheet A has students compare and contrast "Stars" with another of Teasdale's poems, "Night." In Activity Sheet B, students write a "recipe poem" for a star—a star in the sky, a movie star, or some other type of star.

Interdisciplinary Activities

1. **Current events, 1884** Sara Teasdale was born in 1884 in St. Louis, Missouri. Ask your students to check the class time line to identify other poets who were alive at that time. Have them research one of the following questions and report to the class: Who was president the year Teasdale was born? How many states were there in the union at her birth? What was St. Louis like during that time period? (Language Arts, Social Studies, Geography)

2. **Astronomy** This poem naturally lends itself to an astronomy lesson. Many people are unable to identify any of the stars overhead because they do not know north from south or east from west. Ask students to draw a simple compass Rose with north at the top of the compass, south directly below, east to the left of center, and west opposite east. Distribute maps of the United States. Ask questions that will help orient students. For example, ask which is the easternmost state, and let students use their compass Roses to identify Maine. Go on with similar questions until every student knows the directions. Then, determine the directions from your classroom. Position student volunteers around the room, and ask observers to identify their location. Once they have mastered the cardinal directions, ask students to indicate northeast, northwest, etc.

   Explain to the students that the North Star is a very bright star that lies due north in the night sky. For homework, they should locate the North Star after darkness falls that night. If you live in a city where students are not able to view the stars, make arrangements to visit a planetarium where they can see the stars. Prepare them for the visit by discussing the placement of the North Star, the Big Dipper, and the Little Dipper.

   The Glow-in-the-Dark Night Sky Book by Clint Hatchet (New York: Random House, 1988) has clear illustrations of the various constellations. A book of this type would help students get their bearings in the sky. (Geography, Astronomy)

3. **Mythology and constellations** Many of the stars are named after characters in Greek and Roman mythology. Students might enjoy reading a series of myths connected with these "star" characters. Among the characters they might check are Pegasus, the winged horse; Perseus, the Greek hero who killed Medusa; Hercules, the strongest and bravest man on earth; Hydra, a many-headed monster killed by Hercules; and Orion, a hunter killed by Artemis. (Language Arts)

4. **Wishing on a star** Find the words and music to "When You Wish Upon a Star," from the Disney film *Pinocchio*. Ask if anyone knows another star song or poem. Most will know "Star Light, Star Bright." Ask students to write out the words to this well-known verse and then write a paragraph about why they think people wish on stars. (Language Arts, Music)

Activity Sheet A

STUDENT PAGE

Name _____ Date _____

Stars

Here is another of Sara Teasdale's poems. Read the poem. Then answer the following questions. Use the back of this sheet or a separate page for your answers.

> **NIGHT**
>
> *Stars over snow*
>
> *And in the west a planet*
>
> *Swinging below a star—*
>
> *Look for a lovely thing and you will find it.*
>
> *It is not far—*
>
> *It never will be far.*
>
> —Sara Teasdale

1. Why do you think Sara Teasdale named this poem "Night" when it is about stars? Is it that stars are visible only at night? Can you explain the title in any other way?
2. If you were to name this poem, what name would you choose and why?
3. What similarities can you see between the poems "Night" and "Stars"? List at least two.
4. What differences can you find between the two poems?
5. Of the two, which do you like best? Why?

© 2000 J. Weston Walch, Publisher   35   10-Minute Poetry Activities Across the Curriculum

Activity Sheet B   STUDENT PAGE

Name _____ Date _____

Stars: Writing a Recipe

Usually, when we think of a recipe, we think of food preparation. In this activity, you will develop a recipe for something quite different. For example, let's say you were asked to write the recipe for success on a test. You might write:

A RECIPE FOR SUCCESS ON A TEST

1 review of notes   8 hours of sleep

2 phone calls to friends   2 sharp pencils

Combine all the ingredients. Add a careful reading of test questions. Allow to simmer for 45 minutes. Serve the test to the teacher with a smile.

Your assignment is to write a recipe for a star. Remember, there are many types of stars. You can write a recipe for a sports star of some type, a movie star, or a star in the sky. It's up to you. Be sure to name your recipe. List your ingredients. Then provide the directions to be followed.

A Recipe for _____

_____

_____

_____

_____

_____

_____

© 2000 J. Weston Walch, Publisher   36   10-Minute Poetry Activities Across the Curriculum

Name _____ Date _____

Casey at the Bat

The outlook wasn't brilliant for the Mudville nine that day;
The score stood four to two with but one inning more to play.
And then when Cooney died at first, and Barrows did the same,
A sickly silence fell upon the patrons of the game.

A straggling few got up to go in deep despair. The rest
Clung to that hope which springs eternal in the human breast;
They thought if only Casey could but get a whack at that—
We'd put up even money now with Casey at the bat.

But Flynn preceded Casey, as did also Johnnie Blake,
And the former was a lulu and the latter was a cake;
So upon that stricken multitude grim melancholy sat,
For there seemed but little chance of Casey's getting to the bat.

But Flynn let drive a single, to the wonderment of all,
And Blake, the much despisèd, tore the cover off the ball;
And when the dust had lifted, and the men saw what had occurred,
There was Johnnie safe at second and Flynn a-hugging third.

Then from 5,000 throats and more there rose a lusty yell;
It rumbled through the valley, it rattled in the dell;
It knocked upon the mountain and recoiled upon the flat,
For Casey, mighty Casey, was advancing to the bat.

There was ease in Casey's manner as he stepped into his place;
There was pride in Casey's bearing and a smile on Casey's face.
And when, responding to the cheers, he lightly doffed his hat,
No stranger in the crowd could doubt 'twas Casey at the bat.

(continued)

Casey at the Bat (continued)

Ten thousand eyes were on him as he rubbed his hands with dirt;
Five thousand tongues applauded when he wiped them on his shirt.
Then while the writhing pitcher ground the ball into his hip,
Defiance gleamed in Casey's eye, a sneer curled Casey's lip.

And now the leather-covered sphere came hurtling through the air,
And Casey stood a-watching it in haughty grandeur there.
Close by the sturdy batsman the ball unheeded sped—
"That ain't my style," said Casey. "Strike one," the umpire said.

From the benches, black with people, there went up a muffled roar,
Like the beating of the storm-waves on a stern and distant shore.
"Kill him! Kill the umpire!" shouted some one on the stand;
And it's likely they'd have killed him had not Casey raised his hand.

With a smile of Christian charity great Casey's visage shone;
He stilled the rising tumult; he bade the game go on;
He signaled to the pitcher, and once more the spheroid flew;
But Casey still ignored it, and the umpire said, "Strike two."

"Fraud!" cried the maddened thousands, and echo answered fraud;
But one scornful look from Casey and the audience was awed.
They saw his face grow stern and cold, they saw his muscles strain,
And they knew that Casey wouldn't let that ball go by again.

The sneer is gone from Casey's lip, his teeth are clenched in hate;
He pounds with cruel violence his bat upon the plate.
And now the pitcher holds the ball, and now he lets it go,
And now the air is shattered by the force of Casey's blow.

Oh, somewhere in this favored land the sun is shining bright;
The band is playing somewhere, and somewhere hearts are light,
And somewhere men are laughing, and somewhere children shout;
But there is no joy in Mudville—mighty Casey has struck out.

—Ernest Lawrence Thayer

Casey at the Bat

Procedure

"Casey at the Bat" is ideal for choral reading. It is a little long for memorization, although the great-great-grandparents of your students would have easily memorized a piece of this length. Can your students live up to the challenge?

Activity Sheet A has students match some of the unusual or idiomatic terms in the poem with their definitions. Activity Sheet B has students describe Casey's performance from a variety of points of view, including his teammates and the opposing pitcher.

Interdisciplinary Activities

1. **Casey's character** Distribute copies of the poem to your students. Read it aloud to them as they follow along. Ask them to characterize Casey. Help them to do so by asking such questions as: "Was he too arrogant?" "Did people expect too much from him?" "Did you expect him to strike out? Why or why not?" and "How do you think Casey felt at the end of the game? How did people treat him when he walked off the field?" For each answer, insist they offer proof for their answer from the poem.

   Have students write a dialogue between Casey and a fan who had seen the game. Get them to consider the relationship between the two by asking if Casey would apologize, or if the fan would try to make him feel better. Have students share their work with the class. (Language Arts)

2. **Date of the poem** Ask students when they think the poem was written, and have them support their answers with material from the poem. They will probably point out the unfamiliar uses of words like "lulu," "cake," and "spheroid." Before telling your students when it was written, remind them that language is not static; it is always changing. Then, explain that the poem was written in 1888.

3. **Literary map and time line** Ernest Lawrence Thayer was born in Lawrence, Massachusetts, in 1863 and died in Santa Barbara, California in 1940. Add Thayer's name to your time line and your map.

4. **Researching Thayer's contemporaries** Thayer was the son of a well-to-do mill owner. A Harvard graduate, Thayer knew many influential men of the late nineteenth and early twentieth centuries. Ask students to research William James, William Randolph Hearst, and George Syntony, all of whom were Thayer's friends.

5. **Dramatic reading** Assign individual stanzas to students to memorize and act out. Emphasize that this is a dramatic piece; encourage them to "ham it up." The performance should be fun for everyone. (Language Arts)

6. **Casey's Revenge** If students seem interested, read them "Casey's Revenge" (*The Best Loved Poems of the American People*. Hazel Fellemen, comp. Garden City, N.Y.: Doubleday, 1936). Students can learn more about the poem and the poet through the Internet; they can key in either the title of the poem or "Thayer, Ernest." (Language Arts, Technology)

Answers

Activity Sheet A
1. F
2. B
3. G
4. E
5. C
6. A
7. H
8. D

Activity Sheet A

STUDENT PAGE

Name _____ Date _____

Casey at the Bat: Word Play

Match each word with its definition. The words are given in the same order as they appear in the poem. Write the letter in front of the number.

_____ 1. die at first   A. twisting

_____ 2. whack   B. chance

_____ 3. tore the cover off   C. tipped

_____ 4. a-huggin'   D. face

_____ 5. doffed   E. close to

_____ 6. writhing   F. get tagged "out"

_____ 7. leather-covered sphere   G. hit very hard

_____ 8. visage   H. a baseball

© 2000 J. Weston Walch, Publisher — 10-Minute Poetry Activities Across the Curriculum

Activity Sheet B

STUDENT PAGE

Name _____ Date _____

Casey at the Bat

Different people can view the same event or person and come away with very different interpretations. We all interpret situations and people based on our own personal experience. In this activity you are asked to look at Casey's performance in the game from a variety of points of view.

1. What would Casey's mother say about his performance? Remember, this is her son and she is proud of him. _____
_____

2. What would the opposing pitcher say? _____
_____

3. What would one of Casey's teammates say? _____
_____

4. What would a young fan say? _____
_____

5. What would Casey's catcher say? _____
_____

The Eagle

He clasps the crag with crookèd hands;
Close to the sun in lonely lands,
Ring'd with the azure world, he stands.

The wrinkled sea beneath him crawls;
He watches from his mountain walls,
And like a thunderbolt he falls.

—*Alfred, Lord Tennyson*

The Eagle

Procedure

The rhyme scheme of this poem is unlike that of any other poem considered so far. *a-a-a-b-b-b* is fairly unusual. Read the poem aloud to your students and ask them to identify the rhyme scheme. This should be a very easy poem for them to memorize.

Ask students about their overall reaction to this poem. Start out with simple observations, such as how they picture this bird and whether this bird is afraid of his environment. Draw their attention to the sea that "crawls" below him and his dive that is like a thunderbolt. They should notice that the poet has placed the eagle on a par with the sun. The whole poem suggests strength and boldness.

Activity Sheet A has students compare and contrast "The Eagle" and "A Bird Came down the Walk" (on p. 29 of this book). In Activity Sheet B, students match birds with their physical attributes.

Interdisciplinary Activities

1. **Literary map and time line** Alfred, Lord Tennyson was born in Somersby, England, in 1809. He died in 1892, during the reign of Queen Victoria. Add his name to the class time line and to the map. (Social Studies)

2. **Literary techniques** The poet uses a number of recognizable poetic techniques in this poem that your students will find in many other poems. For example, *alliteration* is used in stanza one:

    "<u>c</u>lasps the <u>c</u>rag with <u>c</u>rookèd ..."

    Another device to notice is the *personification* of the eagle. In line one, the poem refers to his crooked "hands," rather than the expected "claws." Ask students to find examples of these literary techniques in other poems they have studied. (Language Arts)

3. **British peerage and poets laureate** The title "Lord" was given to Tennyson when he became poet laureate of England. Assign individual projects in which students research the British peerage. Who are some well-known personages who have titles? Who is England's poet laureate now? Does the United States have a poet laureate? (We do.) (Social Studies, Language Arts)

4. **Physical attributes and habitat** Show pictures of eagles to your students. Point out the size of the eagle's beak and of its claws. What do they suggest about the eagle's eating habits? Students should notice that the bird's feet enable it to grasp its prey, while its beak is well suited for ripping and tearing. Mention that much can be learned about the various species of birds by studying their beaks and feet. Show a picture of a wading bird such as a heron to make this point. If the study of birds is included in your curriculum, this would be an excellent poem to begin such a unit. You might develop a couple of lessons around the feet and beaks of birds. For example, the grosbeaks all have strong, slightly curved beaks because they are seed eaters. Hawks, like the eagle, have strong beaks that enable them to rip flesh apart. Crows have long beaks that enable them to eat almost anything that comes their way. Activity Sheet B is designed to follow up this activity. (Science)

Activity Sheet A

STUDENT PAGE

Name _____ Date _____

The Eagle: Comparing and Contrasting Two Poems

When you **compare** two things, you concentrate on the ways in which they are similar. When you **contrast** two things, you emphasize their differences. For example, if you were to compare two people, you might mention that both are high-school students. If you wanted to contrast them, you might mention that one is a freshman and one is a sophomore.

In this activity you will compare two poems, "The Eagle" and "A Bird Came down the Walk . . ." Your first step will be to fill in the chart below with similarities and differences between the two poems. Based on your findings, decide whether or not you think the poems are more alike than different. On a separate sheet, explain your conclusion. You might begin by writing something like: "Although both of these poems are about birds, they are very different," or "These poems are alike because . . ." In either case, be specific. Back up your thinking with clear statements. Explain your ideas using examples from the chart and from the poem.

As you fill in the chart, consider the use of alliteration, metaphor, simile, rhyme scheme, language, and subject matter.

Compare and Contrast Chart			
	SIMILARITY 1	SIMILARITY 2	SIMILARITY 3
A Bird Came Down the Walk . . .			
The Eagle			
	DIFFERENCE 1	DIFFERENCE 2	DIFFERENCE 3
A Bird Came Down the Walk . . .			
The Eagle			

© 2000 J. Weston Walch, Publisher   44   10-Minute Poetry Activities Across the Curriculum

Activity Sheet B

STUDENT PAGE

Name _____ Date _____

The Eagle

Like other animals, birds have distinct characteristics. They develop skills and physical attributes to suit their habitats. For example, loons are water birds. They have powerful lungs to help them hunt for food under the water.

On the line by each pair of feet, write the name of the bird to which they belong. Before making your decision, remember the bird's usual habitat and activities. Choose from the word list at the left.

eagle

hummingbird

pelican

robin

mallard

Now, on the line by each beak, write the name of the bird to which it belongs. Think about what each bird eats before making your decision.

eagle

hummingbird

pelican

robin

mallard

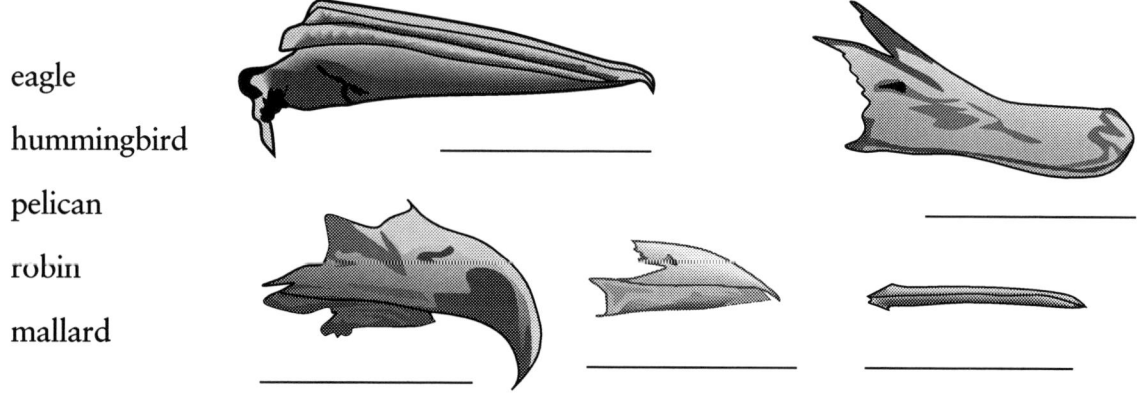

© 2000 J. Weston Walch, Publisher   45   10-Minute Poetry Activities Across the Curriculum

The Mountain and the Squirrel

The mountain and the squirrel

Had a quarrel,

And the former called the latter "Little prig";

Bun replied,

"You are doubtless very big;

But all sorts of things and weather

Must be taken in together

To make up a year,

And a sphere.

And I think it no disgrace

To occupy my place.

If I'm not so large as you,

You are not so small as I,

And not half so spry.

I'll not deny you make

A very pretty squirrel track.

Talents differ; all is well and wisely put;

If I cannot carry forests on my back,

Neither can you crack a nut!"

—*Ralph Waldo Emerson*

The Mountain and the Squirrel

Procedure

Emerson offers the reader wonderful responses to comments about size and difference. If for no other reason than that, the poem is worth memorizing. The rhyme scheme is irregular, so students will have to understand the poem if they are to memorize it. Ask them to establish the setting first. Point out that the mountain speaks only once, when it calls the squirrel "Little prig." From then on, the small squirrel has its say.

Next, emphasize the line, "And I think it no disgrace / To occupy my place." Discuss the meaning of these words with students. They should understand that the squirrel is saying everything has its proper place.

Activity Sheet A asks students to identify some prominent contemporaries of Emerson. Activity Sheet B guides students toward an understanding of their own reactions to the poem.

Interdisciplinary Activities

1. **Literary map and time line** Ralph Waldo Emerson was born in Boston in 1803 and died in 1882. Add his name to your class time line and literary map. Emerson was a powerful influence in American literature and counted among his friends the cultural leaders of Boston. Activity Sheet A will introduce students to some of the famous people of the time. (Social Studies, Language Arts)
2. **Reacting to the poem** Ask students to consider why Emerson chose a squirrel and a mountain as the characters in this poem. Have students brainstorm ideas. Ask students to state and support their reactions to this poem. Some may be put off by the irregular rhyme scheme. Others may find it silly to have a mountain talking. As in past poetry lessons, insist on reasons for their answers. (Language Arts)
3. **Reporting on an event** Ask students to use the events and characters of the poem to write a story. If they had observed the scene, how might they report it to an audience? The more matter-of-factly this is presented, the funnier it should be. (Language Arts)
4. **Point of view** Ask students to write the story from the point of view of one of the characters. Have them imagine what the character would be thinking as the conversation takes place. (Language Arts)
5. **Concord, Massachusetts** Use the Internet to research the community of Concord, Massachusetts. Where is it located? How far is it from Boston? How large is the community? For what is it best known? What famous historical event took place there? What important historical and literary landmarks can be found there? Have students present their findings in class. (Social Studies, Language Arts)

Answers

Activity Sheet A
1. F
2. E
3. G
4. C
5. H
6. D
7. I
8. A
9. J
10. B

Activity Sheet A   **STUDENT PAGE**

Name _____ Date _____

The Mountain and the Squirrel

Ralph Waldo Emerson lived during a particularly turbulent time in American history. He was born in 1803 and died in 1882, so he lived through the Civil War. Below you will find a list of prominent people who lived during this time period. Match each name with the correct description of that person's accomplishments. If you are not sure, use a reference book to check the facts.

_____ 1. Walt Whitman

_____ 2. Jefferson Davis

_____ 3. Harriet Beecher Stowe

_____ 4. Ulysses S. Grant

_____ 5. Clara Barton

_____ 6. Harriet Tubman

_____ 7. Robert E. Lee

_____ 8. Louisa May Alcott

_____ 9. Henry David Thoreau

_____ 10. Abraham Lincoln

A. The author of *Little Women*

B. President of the United States during the Civil War

C. A Union general and later president

D. Helped slaves escape through the Underground Railroad

E. President of the Confederacy

F. A poet who wrote of war experiences

G. The author of *Uncle Tom's Cabin*

H. Founder of the American Red Cross

I. Commander of the Confederate forces

J. The author of *Walden,* which describes the author's time away from the hustle and bustle of life

© 2000 J. Weston Walch, Publisher   48   10-Minute Poetry Activities Across the Curriculum

Activity Sheet B

STUDENT PAGE

Name _____ Date _____

The Mountain and the Squirrel

Did you like "The Mountain and the Squirrel"? Think about how you explain why something pleases you or displeases you? Refer to the following checklist as you reread the poem and then react to each statement. Then use the information you have organized to write a paragraph in which you explain your attitude toward this poem. Begin your paragraph by stating your opinion of the poem. Support your opinion with specific information. Use the back of this sheet or a separate piece of paper.

The poet addressed a specific issue. _____

The poet selected interesting characters to play parts in his poem. _____

The rhyme scheme of the poem made it easy to read. _____

The word choice was simple and clear. _____

The poem made a serious comment on a problem. _____

The poem helped me to see how another person might view the problem. _____

The poem was confusing. _____

The poem was one I would have read no matter where I found it. _____

This kind of poem holds no interest for me. _____

Jabberwocky

'Twas brillig, and the slithy toves
    Did gyre and gimble in the wabe:
All mimsy were the borogoves,
    And the mome raths outgrabe.

"Beware the Jabberwock, my son!
    The jaws that bite, the claws that catch!
Beware the Jubjub bird, and shun
    The frumious Bandersnatch!"

He took his vorpal sword in hand:
    Long time the manxome foe he sought—
So rested he by the Tumtum tree,
    And stood awhile in thought.

And, as in uffish thought he stood,
    The Jabberwock, with eyes of flame,
Came whiffling through the tulgey wood,
    And burbled as it came!

One, two! One, two! And through and through
    The vorpal blade went snicker-snack!
He left it dead, and with its head
    He went galumphing back.

"And hast thou slain the Jabberwock?
    Come to my arms, my beamish boy!
O frabjous day! Callooh! Callay!"
    He chortled in his joy.

'Twas brillig, and the slighy toves
    Did gyre and gimble in the wabe:
All mimsy were the borogoves,
    And the mome raths outgrabe.

—Lewis Carroll

TEACHER PAGE

Jabberwocky

Procedure

Although Lewis Carroll is primarily known as the author of *Alice's Adventures in Wonderland* and *Through the Looking Glass*, he began his career as a lecturer in mathematics at Oxford University. His first published book was *A Syllabus of Plane Algebraical Geometry* in 1860. Point out to students that a love of numbers and a love of words are not antithetical. For more information on Carroll, see pages 18, 26.

Activity Sheet A has students develop a dictionary of the invented words in "Jabberwocky."

Interdisciplinary Activities

1. **Translating "Jabberwocky"** Begin working with the poem by reading the first stanza aloud. You may have to repeat it in order for students to become comfortable with this "foreign language." On your second reading, emphasize the storytelling lilt of the stanzas. Your students should quickly recognize that this is not merely gibberish, but conveys a story. Ask students to describe the setting of the first stanza. In order to do this more easily, show the stanza on an overhead and discuss the underlined words.

    'Twas <u>brillig</u> and the <u>slithy</u> toves

    Did <u>gyre and gimble</u> in the <u>wabe</u>:

    All <u>mimsy</u> were the <u>borogoves</u>,

    And the <u>mome raths outgrabe</u>.

    Ask how the words "slithy" and "mimsy" are similar. Most students should understand that they are adjectives. Have your class define these words. Some students may see the similarity between brilliant and brillig, or they may see it as a noun, e.g., winter, summer, evening. Discuss. Others will mention that slithy sounds a lot like slimy. Go on to discuss "gyre" and "gimble." They are obviously verbs, since there is an auxiliary verb in front of them. "Mimsy" is another descriptive word, while "outgrabe" is another verb. Get students to notice that the position of words in a sentence often indicates what part of speech they are. Go through the stanza a second time and ask students to find words they think are nouns. Since "toves" is described by an adjective, it must be a noun. "Borogoves" is another noun. "Raths" is a noun with the adjective "mome" describing it. Ask students to rewrite the first stanza in English (or another language in which they are competent) and then read their version aloud. Finish the first class on "Jabberwocky" by reading the remainder of the poem out loud to the class. Discuss the major characters in the poem. Students should recognize that a father is speaking to his son, who must face the Jabberwock in battle. List the characters on the board and use them as a starting point for your second day with "Jabberwocky." Continue looking at individual words as you did with the first stanza. (Language Arts, Language Diversity)

2. **Jabberwocky dictionary** Ask students to develop a dictionary of "Jabberwocky" words. The dictionary should be in alphabetical order and include the part of speech, definition, origin, and pronunciation of each word. See Activity Sheet A for guidelines. Complete the activity by making copies for other classes. (Language Arts, Art, Technology)

3. **Comic strip** Ask the artists in your class to develop a comic strip. Each frame can represent a stanza. This strip could be developed into a slide show to present to other classes. (Art, Technology, Language Arts)

4. **Jabberwock masks** Hold a contest in which students make and submit masks of the Jabberwock. (Art)

Activity Sheet A   **STUDENT PAGE**

Name _____   Date _____

Jabberwocky: "Jabberwocky" Dictionary

Here's a list of words from the poem "Jabberwocky." On a separate piece of paper, create a "Jabberwocky" dictionary. For each word, supply a pronunciation guide, part of speech, creative definition, and the origin of the word. You may also illustrate your entry. Refer to the poem for contextual clues that will help you develop a definition. The first one is done for you.

> **Bandersnatch**—(Ban der snach), *n.* 1. A fire-breathing bird that grabs food from weaker birds. 2. A bold, meandering thief. The word's origins are from the Dumblish for thief.

beamish	mimsy
borogoves	mome maths
brillig	outgrabe
callooh	slithy
callay	snicker-snack
frabjous	toves
frumious	tulgey
gyre	tumtum tree
gimble	uffish
Jabberwock	vorpal
jubjub bird	wabe
manxome	

© 2000 J. Weston Walch, Publisher   52   10-Minute Poetry Activities Across the Curriculum

Check

The night was creeping on the ground;
She crept and did not make a sound
Until she reached the tree, and then
She covered it, and stole again
Along the grass beside the wall.

I heard the rustle of her shawl
As she threw blackness everywhere
Upon the sky and ground and air,
And in the room where I was hid:
But no matter what she did
To everything that was without
She could not put my candle out.

So I stared at the night, and she
Stared back solemnly at me.

—*James Stephens*

Teacher Page

The Check

Procedure

James Stephens was born in Dublin, Ireland, in 1882. He began his professional life as a typist in a lawyer's office. His first book, *Insurrections,* was published in 1909. Stephens was among the many Irish literary figures who took part in the Easter Rising of 1916. On that Easter Monday, a group of revolutionaries attempted to secure Irish independence from England. Stephens's view of those events was published in *The Insurrection in Dublin.* In addition to poetry, he wrote plays, novels, and short stories. Stephens left Ireland in 1925 to live in London, where he died in 1950.

Begin your study of this poem by reading it out loud to your class. Encourage students to consider the effectiveness of the images Stephens has created. Do your students see night in the same way as the narrator of this poem?

Activity Sheet A guides students to an understanding of Stephens's use of personification in this poem. In Activity Sheet B, they imagine what the person "Night" might be like, and write a description of him or her.

Interdisciplinary Activities

1. **Literary map and time line** Add Stephens to the time line of poets your class has studied. Ask students to locate and mark Dublin on the map. (Social Studies, Language Arts)

2. **Personification** Stephens uses personification to bring his poem to life. Personification is the technique of ascribing human qualities to animals or inanimate objects. Ask students to complete Activity Sheet A, which follows this lesson. (Language Arts)

3. **Latitude and longitude** Stephens creates a vivid picture of night. Ask students if night falls in Ireland at the same time as it does in your location. Have students compare the longitude and latitude of your location with those of Dublin. Discuss how latitude affects how long the days are and when night falls. (Geography)

4. **Irish folk tales** Find a collection of Irish folk tales in your library. Select one to share with your students. Ask how Irish legends differ from American legends, such as Paul Bunyan or Johnny Appleseed. Students from other countries might enjoy sharing some of the tales of their native lands. This would be an excellent opportunity to discuss the importance that legends play in all cultures. Despite their differences, folktales of different cultures share many features including larger-than-life heroes and heroines, exaggerated accomplishments, and similar plots. (Language Arts, Social Studies)

5. **Rhyme scheme** Have students identify the rhyme scheme used in "Check"—*a-a-b-b*.

Activity Sheet A

STUDENT PAGE

Name _____ Date _____

Check

James Stephens uses both rhyme and personification in this poem. You know that rhyme is the repetition of a sound at the ends of words. Do you know what personification is? Read the example below:

The night was creeping on the ground;

Notice that Stephens says the night "was creeping." "Creeping" is something a person does. The poem describes the night as if it were a person. That is an example of **personification,** giving human qualities to non-humans.

1. Find at least four examples of personification in this poem.
    1. _____
    2. _____
    3. _____
    4. _____

2. Is the night male or female? _____ How do you know? _____
   _____

3. When do you think this poem was written? Support this claim with a quote from the poem. _____
   _____

4. What do you know about the narrator (the "I" of the poem)? _____
   _____

© 2000 J. Weston Walch, Publisher — 10-Minute Poetry Activities Across the Curriculum

Activity Sheet B   STUDENT PAGE

Name _____ Date _____

Check

In the poem "Check," James Stephens speaks as if the night were alive. Imagine that night is a person. What would this person look like? Would night be male or female? Where would night go during the day? Who might his or her friends be? Write a description of Mr. or Ms. Night.

_____

_____

_____

_____

_____

_____

_____

_____

_____

_____

_____

_____

_____

_____

_____

_____

Full Fathom Five...

Full fathom five thy father lies;

    Of his bones are coral made;

Those are pearls that were his eyes;

    Nothing of him that doth fade

But does suffer a sea-change

Into something rich and strange.

Sea-nymphs hourly ring his knell.

        Ding-dong.

Hark! Now I hear 'them

Ding dong, bell!

—*William Shakespeare*

Teacher Page

Full Fathom Five...

Procedure

Introduce this poem by reading it aloud. Emphasize the first line. Students should notice that the alliteration is quite striking. Read it again before discussing the poem. Ask when they think this poem was written and who they think wrote it. After the guesses have played out, mention that this is the oldest poem studied thus far and that it was written to be sung in a sixteenth-century play. Show them a copy of the poem on the overhead and have them look for unfamiliar words as a way of determining when it was written. "Thy," "doth," and "knell" should be picked out immediately as words that are no longer used. Before students lose interest, tell them that the poet is best known as a playwright. Someone should then be able to identify Shakespeare as the poet.

Discuss the poem's topic, the description of a body lost at sea. It is not necessary to discuss the play from which this is taken, although you may want to mention that it is from *The Tempest*.

Activity Sheet A guides students to an understanding of some of the literary techniques used in this poem, as well as some of the unfamiliar words. Activity Sheet B gives students some information about Shakespeare.

Interdisciplinary Activities

1. **Literary map and time line** Shakespeare was born in Stratford-on-Avon, England, in 1564. Ask students to add his name to the literary time line and to the literary map they have been developing. (Language Arts, Geography)

2. **Fathoms as measures** Ask students to look up the word "fathom." Have them calculate how many feet are in five fathoms. (A fathom is equal to six feet.) Tell students that the word "fathom" comes from the Latin *pandere*, "to spread out." It was originally the distance of a person's outstretched arms, from fingertip to fingertip. Have students work in pairs to measure their own "personal fathoms," then compare them to the actual fathom measure of six feet. In "personal fathoms," how far below the water does Antonio, Ferdinand's father, lie? (Math, Language Arts)

3. **Study of coral** Students may be interested to learn more about coral. Ask them to use the Internet or a reference book to verify Shakespeare's scientific knowledge. They should research whether the father's bones could actually become coral. (Yes, because coral is constructed of the skeletons of great numbers of sea animals.) In the past few years, scientists have learned that many of the great coral reefs are disintegrating. A small group of students might like to be responsible for presenting a report on the ecology of coral reefs. (Science)

4. **How pearls are formed** Shakespeare declares: "Those are pearls that were his eyes." Assign another small group to report on how pearls are formed within the shells of oysters. (Science)

Answers

Activity Sheet A

1. full fathom five father; suffer sea-change; something strange; nymphs knell; hark hear
2. a-b-a-b-c-c-d
3. one
4. a bell rung for a funeral
5. No; it is described as archiac.
6. Yes

Activity Sheet B

1. England
2. He was born on April 23, 1564, and died on April 23, 1616.
3. Shakespeare is known to have written 38 plays, so many answers are possible here. Students are most likely to be familiar with just a few, including those named on the activity sheet: *Hamlet, Prince of Denmark; Macbeth; Romeo and Juliet; A Midsummer Night's Dream; Julius Caesar; The Tempest;* and *The Merchant of Venice.*

Activity Sheet A

STUDENT PAGE

Name _____ Date _____

Full Fathom Five . . .

Although Shakespeare wrote many years ago, he used the same literary techniques that you have seen other poets use. For this activity, you will need to know the meaning of the following:

- alliteration
- rhyme scheme
- quotation marks

If you don't know these terms, look them up in the dictionary. Do your work on a separate sheet of paper or on the back of this one.

1. Find three examples of alliteration in the poem.

2. What is the rhyme scheme of the first seven lines?

3. How many speakers does this passage have?

4. What is the "knell" referred to in the poem?

5. Dictionaries provide usage labels to indicate under what circumstances a word is appropriate. For example, although "ain't" is in the dictionary, it is inappropriate for many situations because it is considered slang. Shakespeare uses the word "doth." Is this word appropriate for everyday use? Explain.

6. According to the dictionary, are the words "hark" and "knell" appropriate for everyday use?

7. Do you think that people two hundred years from now will be using the same English words we use? Explain.

© 2000 J. Weston Walch, Publisher

Activity Sheet B **STUDENT PAGE**

Name _____ Date _____

Full Fathom Five...

Some literary experts doubt that one person could have written all the works that are attributed to Shakespeare. Various people have been mentioned as the authors of everything from *Hamlet* to *The Tempest*. Much of this controversy may be because it is hard to understand how a young Englishman of his time could have had the extensive knowledge necessary to write the plays.

Although William Shakespeare's birthday is celebrated on April 23 all over the world, there is no birth record to back up this claim. The only record that exists is of his baptism on April 26, 1564.

William Shakespeare married Anne Hathaway in 1582. The couple had three children, Susanna, Hamnet, and Judith. Hamnet died in boyhood. It is generally believed that Shakespeare left Stratford in 1585 to begin his theater career. Among the plays that brought him fame are *Hamlet, Romeo and Juliet, Julius Caesar, The Tempest,* and *The Merchant of Venice.* Shakespeare died on April 23, 1616.

Answer the following questions about William Shakespeare.

1. In what country was he born? _____
2. What is unusual about his birth and death dates? _____
   _____
   _____
3. Name three of his plays. _____
   _____
   _____

Ozymandias

I met a traveler from an antique land,

Who said: Two vast and trunkless legs of stone

Stand in the desert. Near them, on the sand,

Half sunk, a shattered visage lies, whose frown,

And wrinkled lip, and sneer of cold command,

Tell that its sculptor well those passions read

Which yet survive, stamped on these lifeless things,

The hand that mocked them, and the heart that fed:

And on the pedestal these words appear:

"My name is Ozymandias, king of kings:

Look on my works, ye Mighty, and despair!"

Nothing beside remains. Round the decay

Of that colossal wreck, boundless and bare

The lone and level sands stretch far away.

—*Percy Bysshe Shelley*

Teacher Page

Ozymandias

Procedure

This poem should be both heard and seen. Make a copy for each student or show the poem on an overhead. The title of the poem may seem a little formidable to middle-school students, so practice its pronunciation with them: oz-i-man-de-as. Read it through with them a couple of times and ask for their reactions. Probably, most students will miss the message of the poem: Nothing people build will necessarily stand forever. All-powerful kings die and their power dies with them.

Students may be interested to know that this poem is an example of a sonnet, which means it has fourteen lines and a predictable rhyme scheme.

Activity Sheet A will help students understand what Shelley is saying in this poem. Activity Sheet B is for students to use as they investigate statues in your area that honor an individual or a group.

Interdisciplinary Activities

1. **Literary map and time line** Add Shelley to the time line and literary map that your class has been developing. (Language Arts, Geography)
2. **The Shelleys and English society** Percy Bysshe Shelley lived from 1792 to 1822. He was born in England, where he was a close friend of another famous poet, Lord Byron. Shelley was married to Mary Wollstonecraft Shelley, who wrote a novel that will be familiar to your students, *Frankenstein*. Students might enjoy researching the lives of the Shelleys, who led unconventional lives during a very conventional time period. You might ask students to find out why these two people did not fit into proper English society. (Language Arts, Social Studies)
3. **King Ramses II** "Ozymandias" is the Greek name for King Ramses II of Egypt. Ask students to research his life, using both the Internet and reference books. Ask that they locate the site of the king's tomb on a map. They can present their findings orally. (Language Arts, Social Studies, Technology, Geography)
4. **Tyrants today** The world has known many other tyrants like Ozymandias. Ask students to scan local news magazines and papers to discover if any such tyrants are in power anywhere in the world today. This would be a good way of showing students that though centuries may separate them from Ozymandias, human qualities are ageless. (Social Studies, Language Arts, Current Events)
5. **Statues in your area** What statues exist in your community to symbolize the accomplishments of individuals? Ask students to carry out an "archaeological search" of their community. This will not require any digging, except for digging up facts. Activity Sheet B will help get students started on this project. (Social Studies, Math)

Answers

Activity Sheet A
1. Narrator: line 1
   Traveler: lines 2–9, 12–14
   Ozymandias: lines 10–11
2. half sunk, shattered
3. (a) "an antique land" suggest an older civilization than England's.
   (b) "the lone and level sands"—there are no major deserts in Europe.
   (c) "Look on my works . . . and despair."
   (d) All Ozymandias' works had been swept away.
4. The visage has a frown, wrinkled lip, a sneer.

Activity Sheet A

STUDENT PAGE

Name _____ Date _____

Ozymandias

Answer each of the following questions by referring to the poem. Write your answers on a separate sheet of paper or on the back of this one.

1. There are three speakers in this poem. One is the narrator. The second is the "traveler." The third is Ozymandias. Where do the narrator's words begin and end? Which lines are spoken by the "traveler"? Which lines belong to Ozymandias?

2. Describe the condition of the stone statue the "traveler" saw.

3. What support can you find in the poem for the following statements:

    (a) The "traveler" was far from England.

    (b) He was not in Europe.

    (c) Ozymandias thought himself to be all-powerful.

    (d) Time was not Ozymandias's friend.

4. What contextual clues tell you that the word *visage* must mean "face"?

5. In addition to the "traveler" and the king, another person's view is expressed in this poem. Who is it?

6. How did the sculptor show his feelings about the king?

7. What is the narrator's attitude toward the traveler?

8. What is the traveler's attitude toward Ozymandias?

Activity Sheet B   **STUDENT PAGE**

Name _____ Date _____

Ozymandias

You are going on an "archaeological" search of your neighborhood or community. Your job is to locate any statues that were erected in honor of an individual or a group. You may also find that some individuals or events are commemorated by plaques on buildings. For each statue or plaque you find, answer the following questions. You may have to go to your local library to get some of these facts.

1. What name or names appear on the statue or plaque? _____
   _____

2. What did this individual or group accomplish? Why did their peers remember them in this way? _____
   _____

3. When was this statue or plaque raised? _____

4. Describe the plaque or statue. Include its height, and, if possible, a photograph or drawing. _____
   _____

5. Ask three individuals in your community what they know about your "find." Record their statements below. _____
   _____
   _____
   _____
   _____
   _____
   _____
   _____

In Flanders Fields

In Flanders fields the poppies blow
Between the crosses, row on row,
    That mark our place; and in the sky
    The larks, still bravely singing, fly
Scarce heard amid the guns below.

We are the Dead. Short days ago
We lived, felt dawn, saw sunset glow,
    Loved, and were loved, and now we lie
    In Flanders fields.

Take up our quarrel with the foe:
To you from failing hands we throw
    The torch; be yours to hold it high.
    If ye break faith with us who die
We shall not sleep, though poppies grow
    In Flanders fields.

—John McCrae

TEACHER PAGE

In Flanders Fields

Procedure

John McCrae was a Canadian physician who served in the medical corps during World War I. Deeply moved by the death and destruction he saw around him, he wrote "In Flanders Fields." A young sergeant-major, Cyril Allinson, came upon McCrae as he was writing. When McCrae finished, he gave the poem to Allinson to read. Later, McCrae threw the poem away because he was dissatisfied with it. A fellow officer found it and sent it to English newspapers. The magazine *Punch* published it in 1915.

In Activity Sheet A, students compare and contrast "In Flanders Fields" and E. A. Robinson's "The Dark Hills" (on page 21 of this book). Activity Sheet B directs students to research three well-known songs and to determine what event or person each is associated with.

Interdisciplinary Activities

1. **Poet's attitude to war** Begin your discussion by asking students what the general tone of the poem is. Most will recognize its sadness. Have them identify the contrasts McCrae presents in the first stanza. For example, blowing poppies, which signify life and beauty, contrast with crosses, which suggest death. Additionally, the bravely singing and flying birds offer a stark change from the guns below.

    The second stanza continues in the same tone, as the dead speak, but changes in the third. Ask students to determine the poet's attitude toward war. (Language Arts, Social Studies)

2. **Literary map and time line** John McCrae was born in 1872 in Guelph, Ontario, Canada. He died in France in 1918 from pneumonia three years after writing this poem. Add his name to your classroom literary map and time line. (Social Studies, Language Arts, Geography)

3. **Rondo in music, rondeau in verse** This poem is written as a "rondeau," which is a lyric poem containing a refrain (much as in a ballad). In this poem, the line *In Flanders fields* is repeated. Music students will enjoy knowing that in music a "rondeau" or "rondo" is often the last movement of a sonata. Solicit a volunteer to find an example of a rondo to play for the class. A music teacher might enjoy working with you on the comparison with a musical rondo. (Music)

4. **McCrae, Flanders, and WWI** If students ask why McCrae wrote of poppies, explain that poppies grow in uprooted soil, so battlefields provide them with the necessary conditions. McCrae's description of the crosses and poppies is an accurate one. Assign a group of students to research the battle that took place in Flanders during World War I. Reference books and the Internet will furnish a good deal of information. They should also research McCrae himself. (Language Arts, Social Studies, Horticulture)

5. **Paintings of poppies** Many artists have painted poppies. An interesting contrast can be found between the French artist Claude Monet's painting of a poppy field and American Georgia O'Keeffe's "Poppy." Monet was an impressionist, and his poppy field attempts to re-create the experience of seeing the field, rather than a clear painting of poppies. O'Keeffe's, on the other hand, is a realistic representation of a single poppy. As another point of comparison, compare both paintings to a field guide's illustration of a poppy. (Art, Art History)

Answers

Activity Sheet B

"The Star-Spangled Banner"—the shelling of Fort McHenry during the War of 1812; "Over There"—World War I; "Blowin' in the Wind"—the Civil Rights Movement; "Happy Days are Here Again"—the Great Depression, FDR; "When Johnny Comes Marching Home Again"—the Civil War; "Where Have All the Flowers Gone?"—the Vietnam War; "Brother, Can You Spare a Dime?"—the Great Depression

Activity Sheet A

STUDENT PAGE

Name _____ Date _____

In Flanders Fields

In this activity sheet, compare and contrast John McCrae's "In Flanders Fields" and E. A. Robinson's "The Dark Hills."

1. How are the settings of the two poems alike? How are they different? ____
   _____
   _____

2. What is the rhyme scheme of "In Flanders Fields"? How does it differ from that of "The Dark Hill"? _____
   _____

3. Why do you think both poets use the sunset as one of their images?
   _____
   _____

4. What colors do you think of when you read "In Flanders Fields" and "The Dark Hill"? How do the colors you imagine relate to each poem's tone? Is one poem sadder than the other? How do you know? Support your answer with words from the poems. _____
   _____
   _____

5. If you were to draw a picture of "In Flanders Fields," what would you include in your picture? _____

6. If you were going to illustrate "The Dark Hills," what would you include in your picture? _____

7. Which of these two poems do you prefer? Why? _____
   _____

© 2000 J. Weston Walch, Publisher   67   10-Minute Poetry Activities Across the Curriculum

Activity Sheet B   STUDENT PAGE

Name _____ Date _____

In Flanders Fields

Songs are often associated with important moments. With which events or people is each of the following songs associated. You can find information on the Internet or in reference books. Select three songs to research. Then, on a separate piece of paper, answer the questions below about each one.

> **Songs:**
> "The Star-Spangled Banner"
> "Over There"
> "Blowin' in the Wind"
> "Happy Days Are Here Again"
> "When Johnny Comes Marching Home Again"
> "Where Have All the Flowers Gone?"
> "Brother, Can You Spare a Dime?"

1. What is the name of the song?
2. With what event or person is this song associated?
3. What connection can you see between the event and the lyrics of the song?
4. As you know, McCrae's poem was written on a battlefield. Where was this song written?
5. Where did you find your information? If you were given this kind of assignment again, how would you approach it?

I'm Nobody! Who Are You?

I'm nobody! Who Are You?

Are you—nobody—too?

Then there's a pair of us—don't tell!

They'd banish us—you know!

How dreary—to be—somebody!

How public, like a frog—

To tell your name—the livelong day—

To an admiring Bog!

—*Emily Dickinson*

Teacher Page

I'm Nobody! Who Are You?

Procedure

Because of the regular rhyme scheme, this is an easy poem for students to memorize. Remind them of the biographical information in Lesson Eight, and connect this poem with the fact that Emily Dickinson retreated from people outside of her family after 1853. She literally refused to be a "public" person.

This poem is an ideal way to teach irony of situation. Although Dickinson did not wish to promote her name, it has lived on for more than 150 years.

Emily Dickinson's home is located at 280 Main Street in Amherst, Massachusetts. If any of your students chance to visit New England, this would be a wonderful side trip. Not only are many of the rooms open to visitors, but students can see some of the trees and hedges Dickinson would have known. (Call Amherst College or the Amherst Chamber of Commerce for more information.)

Activity Sheet A guides students to learn more about frogs and toads. Activity Sheet B gives students some of Dickinson's characteristics and directs them to think of a job that would be appropriate for her.

Interdisciplinary Activities

1. **Literary map and time line** If you have not already done so, add Emily Dickinson's name to your class time line and identify her birthplace, Amherst, on the classroom literary map. (Geography)

2. **Dickinson's retreat** Hundreds of scholars have addressed the question, "Why did Dickinson retreat to her home?" However, there is no definitive answer to the puzzle. This would make a good project for a group of students who are interested in doing a little research. Ask them to prepare a written report that can be presented to the class. (Language Arts, Technology, Speaking)

3. **Emily Dickinson time line** Dickinson was not always a hermit. She left home when she was 17 to attend Mt. Holyoke Seminary. Ask a group of students to prepare a time line that shows Emily's activities from her birth until her death in May of 1886. The Internet can supply the necessary information. (Technology, Social Studies)

4. **Poem illustration** Ask students to select one line of the poem to illustrate. Under the illustration they are to write the line. Arrange their work around the classroom with the lines in correct sequence. (Art)

Activity Sheet A

STUDENT PAGE

Name _____ Date _____

I'm Nobody! Who Are You?

Emily Dickinson often wrote about nature. In this poem, she writes of frogs and bogs, not often the subjects of poetry. She was well aware of all that was around her.

Do you notice the details that make up your environment? Do you know the difference between a frog and a toad? They are different, yet many of us never take the time to identify them accurately. Using the Internet or a reference book, investigate the worlds of frogs and toads by answering the following questions. Your first step is to identify the statement as true or false. The second step is to test your answer by checking with a reference book or the Internet. Support your answer by quoting from your source.

1. Frogs and toads live in the same habitats.   T   F   _____
   _____

2. Frogs are omnivores.   T   F   _____

3. Toads are herbivores.   T   F   _____

4. Frogs have smooth skins.   T   F   _____
   _____

5. Toads spend time away from water.   T   F   _____
   _____

6. Frogs and toads are amphibians.   T   F   _____
   _____

7. Frogs do not have ears.   T   F   _____

8. Frogs and toads are primarily nocturnal.   T   F   _____
   _____

9. Some frogs are capable of poisoning their enemies.   T   F   _____
   _____

10. Frogs legs are considered a delicacy in some areas of the world.   T   F
    _____

© 2000 J. Weston Walch, Publisher   71   10-Minute Poetry Activities Across the Curriculum

Activity Sheet B

STUDENT PAGE

Name _____ Date _____

I'm Nobody! Who Are You?

Emily Dickinson lived at a time when young women were expected to remain at home until they married. Emily Dickinson never married. If she were alive today, things would be different. She would be expected to leave home and earn her own living.

Look at the list below of Dickinson's qualifications. Add any more that you have learned about. Then, identify the perfect job for Dickinson. Explain why this would be a good job for her.

Qualifications:

Enjoys nature.
Prefers a quiet and calm environment.
Is familiar with ancient history.
Plays the piano.
Reads well.
Has read the classical writers.
Is agile.
Can make excellent gingerbread.
Has a way with words.
Can do light housework.

The job: _____

Because: _____

_____

© 2000 J. Weston Walch, Publisher　　　72　　　10-Minute Poetry Activities Across the Curriculum

The Golf Links

The golf links lie so near the mill
That almost every day
The laboring children can look out
And see the men at play.

—*Sarah N. Cleghorn*

TEACHER PAGE

The Golf Links

Procedure

This poem is a perfect example of the power of poetry. In four simple lines, Sarah N. Cleghorn clearly portrays the plight of mill children. Child labor may not be an issue for your students, but even in the United States today, young children spend their days performing routine tasks. In many situations, the money children can earn is essential to the survival of their families. But children without a childhood are children without hope. In this poem, Cleghorn is addressing the lives of children who, in the nineteenth and early twentieth centuries, were a recognized part of the work force in mills all around this country.

Begin work on this poem by simply discussing the lines with your students. Many students may be able to relate to the poem from first-hand experience. Farm children, especially, are accustomed to helping with the work of a farm. City children may know of young people who spend their lives sewing or doing other kinds of manual labor. You may find that some students would prefer to work rather than attend school. This will offer you an opportunity to discuss the benefits of education for those who have long-term goals.

Activity Sheet A directs students to compare and contrast "The Golf Links" and "The Song of the Shirt," a poem by Thomas Hood (included on the activity sheet). Activity Sheet B has students imagine what their lives would have been like as factory workers in the 1840s.

Interdisciplinary Activities

1. **Literary map and time line** Sarah Norcliffe Cleghorn was born in 1876 in Norfolk, Virginia, but spent her childhood in Manchester, Vermont. She was taught at home before attending the Burr and Burton Seminary in Manchester. In 1895, she attended Radcliffe College for one year. Although she never graduated from college, she went on to teach at Vassar. "The Golf Links" was written after Cleghorn saw children working in a cotton factory located next to a golf course. Child labor became one of the many causes in which she was involved. Add Cleghorn's birth date to the classroom's time line and her name to the literary map. (Geography, Language Arts)

2. **Early technology** Have students investigate the mechanics that powered mills. Two excellent sources are *Mill* by David Macaulay (Boston: Houghton Mifflin, 1983) and *Diary of an Early American Boy, Noah Blake, 1805* by Eric Sloane (New York: W. Funk, 1962). (Technology, Social Studies)

3. **Early mill field trip** The remains of early mills can still be found in many areas. Arrange a field trip to the site of an early mill, or contact the local historical society to find out if any of its members can tell your class of the part mills played in your community. (History, Technology)

4. **Letter to the editor** Ask students to respond to the poem by writing a letter to the editor stating their views on child labor. There are two ways to approach this assignment, either as a reaction to the problem as it existed in the late nineteenth and early twentieth centuries or as a response to child labor today. (Language Arts, History, Current Events)

5. **Mills and the environment** The mills polluted the rivers and streams of this country at a time when people did not recognize the danger this technology posed for the environment. Fortunately, steps have been taken to remedy some of the damage done, and throughout the country, schools have participated directly in cleaning up local rivers and streams. The story of one such cleanup can be found in *Come Back, Salmon* by Molly Cone (San Francisco: Sierra Club Books for Children, 1992). Is there a stream or river in your area that needs to be cleaned up? If so, this book will give you some ideas on starting such a project. You might also ask your class to begin to develop a news bulletin board, where students can post information on current environmental problems. (Language Arts, Science)

Activity Sheet A

STUDENT PAGE

Name _____ Date _____

The Golf Links

The following poem was written by Thomas Hood, who lived from 1799 to 1845. Compare and contrast this poem with Sarah N. Cleghorn's. Write your answers on the back of this sheet, or on another piece of paper.

> **THE SONG OF THE SHIRT**
>
> *Work—Work—Work,*
> *Till the brain begins to swim;*
> *Work—work—work,*
> *Till the eyes are heavy and dim!*
> *Seam, and gusset, and band,*
> *Band, and gusset, and seam,*
> *Till over the buttons I fall asleep,*
> *And sew them on in a dream!*
>
> —Thomas Hood

1. Who is the narrator of this poem? Who is the narrator of Cleghorn's poem?
2. What is the setting of each poem?
3. Which do you find the most powerful? Why?
4. How many years separate the two poems?
5. A second stanza to this poem makes it clear that a shirt is being made. What clues can you find in the first stanza that a shirt is being sewn?
6. List two ways in which these poems are different. List two ways in which they are alike.

Activity Sheet B   STUDENT PAGE

Name _____ Date _____

The Golf Links

In 1843, it was not unusual for children working in cotton mills to be up by 5:00 A.M. and at their machines soon after. Breakfast usually followed two hours of work. Children were given a half hour for lunch. They continued to work until as late as 7:00 P.M. Supper was served at the end of the work day. It consisted of foods such as beans, flapjacks, potatoes, and other heavy foods. Many of these workers had left their farm homes. They were unused to the conditions they found in crowded boarding houses, where dozens of people shared limited space. Imagine going from green fields, fresh water, and fresh vegetables to the confusion of life in a mill town.

How do you think you would feel if you suddenly found yourself in new surroundings where you were expected to work a 12-hour day? Remember, both boys and girls worked these kinds of hours. Write the journal entry of a young person who has just completed the workday described. Begin by jotting down the answers to the following questions. Then write your journal entry on the back of this sheet or on a separate piece of paper.

1. How would you feel physically? _____
   _____

2. How would you feel mentally? _____
   _____

3. What would your attitude be toward the others around you? _____
   _____

4. How would you feel about "the men at play"? (Reread "The Golf Links.")
   _____

5. What would your thoughts be about the future? _____
   _____

6. What would your goals be? _____
   _____

© 2000 J. Weston Walch, Publisher   76   10-Minute Poetry Activities Across the Curriculum

Name _____ Date _____

Dust of Snow

The way a crow

Shook down on me

The dust of snow

From a hemlock tree

Has given my heart

A change of mood

And saved some part

Of a day I had rued.

—Robert Frost

TEACHER PAGE

Dust of Snow

Procedure

Although Robert Frost is considered a New England poet, he was born in San Francisco in 1874 and moved east in 1885. Frost attended Dartmouth and Harvard briefly and worked at a variety of jobs. He tried farming in New Hampshire but met with failure. He was a poet, but his poetic endeavors could not feed his family. Frustrated with the reception of his poetry in America, he went to England in 1912. Three years later he returned to America, and the Frost legend was born.

Some of your students may be familiar with Frost. Begin your work on this poem by asking what they associate with his name. Explain that Frost was particularly skillful at pointing out the significance of nature in our lives. Ask them what he is saying in this poem. Even students who find poetry difficult should recognize Frost's message: little events in daily life can change the way we see the world. Although a simple message, it is nonetheless an important one for students to learn. Life is made up of little things, and we need to be able to recognize their importance and to grow as a result of that recognition.

Activity Sheet A directs students to create their own poems about something that gives them pleasure. Activity Sheet B has students identify the differences and similarities among several different evergreen trees.

Interdisciplinary Activities

1. **Poem illustration** Ask students to draw a picture representing each line of this poem. This will act as a cue for memorization. The first four lines could be illustrated by a crow, falling snow, more snow, and a tree, respectively. The second stanza should be just as easy. The artists in your class will enjoy this activity. Those who have limited faith in their abilities can use stick figures. (Language Arts, Art)

2. **Investigating crows** Since a crow plays a prominent part in this poem, give your students some information on these birds. Then ask them to find a fascinating crow fact to share with the class. To rouse their interest, explain that crows have many interesting characteristics. For example, they can adapt to many environments, from city malls to corn fields; they are playful and have been observed playing tug-of-war; they mate for life; and some crows are able to mimic the human voice. *Bird Brains* by Candace Savage (San Francisco: Sierra Club Book, 1995) has additional information and pictures of crows, ravens, magpies, and jackdaws, all of which demonstrate some of the characteristics described above. (Science)

3. **Hemlock trees** Since the hemlock tree figures prominently in the first stanza, this poem provides an ideal opportunity for students to learn about a tree that grows in many parts of North America. See Activity Sheet B. (Science)

4. **Literary map and time line** Ask students to add Frost to the classroom's literary map and time line. (Language Arts, Social Studies)

5. **Robert Frost afternoon** Gather a collection of poetry anthologies from the library. Ask each student to select another Frost poem they enjoy. Set a date for "An Afternoon with Robert Frost." During this afternoon, students will read the poems they selected. If possible, take the opportunity to help kids develop "party manners." Provide cookies and juice. Perhaps some parents would be willing to bake treats or supply napkins and cups. Make it a special occasion by discussing the behavior you expect from each student. (Language Arts, Social Studies, Etiquette)

Activity Sheet A

STUDENT PAGE

Name _____ Date _____

Dust of Snow

Use Frost's poem as a beginning for your own writing. Think about a simple event that makes you feel good. Possibilities include the smile of recognition a friend gives you, the pleasure of making a basket, getting a good grade, the first delectable bite of a piece of pizza, or the sound of the dismissal bell at the end of the day. Everyone has something! Make a list of the little things that please you.

1. _____
2. _____
3. _____
4. _____

Now choose one to write about. You only need to write one stanza, unless inspiration hits you and you want to add a second. If you have trouble getting started, quickly list the feelings and thoughts you link to each of your "little things." To begin your poem, reread "Dust of Snow" and use it as your model. Fill in the blanks. Then write a final draft on a separate sheet of paper. Don't forget a title.

TITLE _____

The way _____ (a noun)
_____ (an action word and a phrase)
_____ (an action word describing the feeling)
_____ (a summary statement)

Example: The way a basket
Shoots through the hoop
Makes me happy
If only for a moment.

© 2000 J. Weston Walch, Publisher   79   10-Minute Poetry Activities Across the Curriculum

Activity Sheet B

STUDENT PAGE

Name _____ Date _____

Dust of Snow

As you read "Dust of Snow," did you wonder why Robert Frost selected a hemlock tree rather than an apple, oak, or maple? One reason may be that he wanted to use a common tree or one that is green year-round. The hemlock tree is a conifer, because it does not lose its leaves in winter. Another name for conifers is "evergreens." Hemlocks grow in many parts of North America. Does it grow where you live? Consult a guide to your state's trees for the answer to this question. Hemlocks are easy to identify. Their needles are flat and attached to a tiny stem, which in turn is attached to a peg-like base. Examine the drawing at the right. Notice the tiny stem and the blunt points of the needles.

Compare the hemlock to the drawings below. Then, using the given clues, identify these other conifers.

1. Needles in clusters of two to five.   pine

2. Needles with four sides and sharp points.   spruce

3. Scale-like needles.   cedar

Which of these conifers grow in your area? _____

© 2000 J. Weston Walch, Publisher   80   10-Minute Poetry Activities Across the Curriculum

Overheard on a Saltmarsh

Nymph, nymph, what are your beads?
    Green glass, goblin. Why do you stare at them?
Give them me.
        No.
Give them me. Give them me.
        No.
Then I will howl all night in the reeds,
Lie in the mud and howl for them.

Goblin, why do you love them so?

They are better than stars or water,
Better than voices of winds that sing,
Better than any man's fair daughter,
Your green glass beads on a silver ring.

Hush, I stole them out of the moon.

Give me your beads, I desire them.
        No.
I will howl in a deep lagoon
For your green glass beads, I love them so.
Give them me. Give them.
        No.

—*Saki (H. H. Munro)*

Teacher Page

Overheard on a Saltmarsh

Procedure

This is one of the strangest poems in this collection. It may be that this is not a poem for the entire class, but is just the thing for students who enjoy fantasy. Whether you decide to use it with the entire class or with a small group (or individual), begin by reading the poem out loud. Ask for reactions to the poem. Many students will comment on its strangeness. Ask them to identify how many individuals play a part in this poem. Be sure that students understand it is a conversation between a nymph and a goblin before reading it again. This poem has no deep meaning. The pleasure in it is derived from the unlikely characters and the words.

Activity Sheet A directs students to learn more about Saki. Activity Sheet B guides students as they examine the poem more closely.

Interdisciplinary Activities

1. **Literary map and time line** Hector Hugh Munro chose as his pen name "Saki." He was born in Akyab, Burma, in 1870, but his early childhood was spent in Barnstaple, England. His father was stationed in India. One of three children, Munro was brought up by his aunts and grandmother. The Munro children spent little time with other children and for excitement relied on the visits of their uncle, trips to their mother's relatives, and the once-in-four-years visits of their father. It must have been a lonely childhood. When Saki was 23, he spent 13 months in Burma as a member of the military police. Upon his return to England, he began his writing career. He enlisted in the army in 1915 and was sent to France, where he was killed by a sniper on November 13, 1916. Add Saki's name to your literary time line and his birth place to your literary map. Find the locations of Saki's various homes. (Social Studies, Language Arts, Geography)

2. **Saki's short stories** Saki wrote a number of short stories. Interested students might like to read some of these stories. "The Open Door" is a good place to start. In the story, a young girl convinces a gullible young man that a garden door is kept open for the return of relatives who had been killed three years before. (Language Arts)

3. **Salt marshes I** Salt marshes are intriguing places where tidal water and river water meet. The plants that live in these marshes must adapt to a semi-aquatic environment. When the tide is in, the plants stand in a mixture of salt and fresh water. Even after the tide recedes, the soil contains a heavy concentration of saline. To make the point that salt and plants do not always mix, take two cuttings from a geranium or other green plant. Place one cutting in fresh water and the other in water mixed with one teaspoon of salt. Ask students to observe and record what happens to these plants over a period of several days. (Science)

4. **Salt marshes II** Ask students to locate the saltmarsh closest to their community. In order to do this, they will first have to find out where saltmarshes are located and then figure the distance from their hometown. If you live in an area where there is a salt marsh, a local expert might be willing to discuss its unique environment with your students. (Math, Science)

5. **Poem background** Ask students to write a paragraph in which they explain the background of this poem. In their paragraphs they should deal with the following questions as well as other ideas they find interesting:
   1. Where did the nymph get the green glass beads?
   2. What is she doing in the salt marsh?
   3. Where is this salt marsh located?
   4. Why does the goblin want the beads?
   5. Who overhears the conversation? (Writing)

Answers

Activity Sheet A
1. from the *Rubaiyat* of Omar Khayyam.
2. his aunts
3. Queen Victoria
4. *The Westminster Alice* (*Alice's Adventures in Wonderland*, by Lewis Carroll); *Not so Stories* (*Just So Stories*, Rudyard Kipling)
5. the Balkans, Warsaw, St. Petersburg, Paris
6. Answers will vary.
7. Myanmar

Activity Sheet A

STUDENT PAGE

Name _____ Date _____

Overheard on a Saltmarsh

Refer to the Internet or reference materials to answer the following questions which relate to Saki (H. H. Munro).

1. Where did Saki get his pen name? _____
_____

2. On whom did Saki base many of the characters in his short stories?
_____

3. Who ruled England during most of Munro's lifetime? _____
_____

4. Munro published two works whose titles referred to works by other authors. What works were referred to? Who were their authors?
_____
_____

5. Munro was a correspondent for a newspaper, the *Morning Post*. Name three places his assignments took him. _____
_____

6. Which of the poems you have worked with do you think Munro would most like? Explain your answer. _____
_____
_____
_____

7. Munro was born in Burma. What is that country called today? _____
_____

Activity Sheet B   **STUDENT PAGE**

Name _____ Date _____

Overheard on a Saltmarsh: Taking a Closer Look at the Poem

1. In what way is the structure of this poem different from others we have studied? _____
   _____

2. What letter's sound dominates the first six lines? What effect does this have on the reader? _____
   _____

3. The goblin is made to sound quite wild. List the words that create this effect.
   _____

4. How does Saki tell us that the nymph has some unusual power? _____
   _____
   _____

5. What characteristics of a salt marsh are mentioned in the poem? _____
   _____

6. Is the nymph afraid of the goblin? How do you know? _____
   _____
   _____

7. If Munro had not called this poem "Overheard on a Saltmarsh," would we have known there was someone listening? Explain. _____
   _____

8. Would you have liked another title? Make a suggestion. _____
   _____

The Bee

How doth the little busy bee
    Improve each shining hour,
And gather honey all the day
    From every opening flower!

How skillfully she builds her cell!
    How neat she spreads the wax!
And labors hard to store it well
    With the sweet food she makes.

In works of labor or of skill
    I would be busy too;
For Satan finds some mischief still
    For idle hands to do.

In books, or work, or healthful play,
    Let my first years be past;
That I may give for every day
    Some good account at last.

—*Isaac Watts*

> **TEACHER PAGE**

The Bee

Procedure

Your students will be quick to see that "The Bee" comes from another era. Although it may be dated, it suggests a useful path. Read the poem aloud to your students and then show it on an overhead. Ask them when they think this poem was written, insisting that they give reasons for their answers. Among the reasons you should get are word choice ("doth") and the message of the poem (not to waste time). Tell them that the poem was written in the seventeenth century by Isaac Watts, who is best known for writing over 600 hymns. Ask what there is about the poem that suggests the poet was a religious person. They should see that the message of the poem is that by keeping busy like the bee, we will keep out of mischief. Ask them whether they agree.

Activity Sheet A asks students to write a letter to the editor explaining why bees are important. Activity Sheet B has students take on the role of a lazy bee who faces expulsion from the hive and must convince the queen to let him or her stay.

Interdisciplinary Activities

1. **Literary map and time line** Add Isaac Watts to the classroom time line and the literary map. Watts was born in 1674, in Southampton, England, and died in 1748. He was a very intelligent child and began to study Latin when he was four years old. Later, he learned Greek, Hebrew, and French. According to one story, Watts was able to converse in rhyme, a habit his father detested and tried to stop by whipping the boy. As he was being struck, the young Isaac reportedly said:

   > O father, do some pity take
   > And I will no more verses make.

   (Language Arts, Social Studies, Geography)

2. **Researching Isaac Watts** Ask students to learn more about Isaac Watts by researching his life on the Internet and in reference books. (Technology)

3. **Bee sting allergies** Many people are allergic to bee stings. Invite the school nurse or a student who suffers from this allergy to talk to your class about the problem. Allergies can be life-threatening and students should understand the body's reaction to allergens. (Science, Health)

4. **Bee-related words** Ask students to collect "bee" songs, expressions, and titles. Start them off with the expressions "busy as a bee" and "the bee's knees" (a popular phrase of the 1930s meaning "terrific") and the musical piece "Flight of the Bumblebee." Any bee-related word is fair game. (Language Arts, Music)

5. **Beeswax** Explain that the best candles are made of beeswax. Ask a student to research how the wax is harvested. (Science)

6. **Compare and contrast: Lewis Carroll** Lewis Carrol's poem "How Doth the Little Crocodile" (page 25 of this book) is a parody of "The Bee." Have students compare and contrast the two poems.

Activity Sheet A

STUDENT PAGE

Name _____ Date _____

The Bee

Did you know that honeybees are essential to the development of many of the foods that we eat? Many fruits—melons, apples, strawberries, blueberries—must be pollinated for the fruit to ripen. Even beef depends on bees. Cows need alfalfa and legumes for protein in their diets. Guess what alfalfa and legumes need to produce seed for another year? You've got it: bees!

Although some people have to stay away from bees for their own safety, we should all be grateful to them for making our world a fruitful place. Emily Dickinson's poem sums it up well:

To make a prairie it takes a clover and one bee,

Write a letter to the editor of your local paper explaining why bees are important. Use a separate sheet of paper. Your goal is to make people aware of the role bees play. Research will give you the facts you need to accomplish that goal.

Activity Sheet B

Name _____ Date _____

The Bee

    The bee is known as an industrious insect, one who has a job and is always doing it. Pretend that you are an unlikely bee—one that doesn't want to work. You are a member of a large hive where everyone buzzes around all day. Your family has become more and more unhappy with your attitude toward work. As a matter of fact, the queen bee is ready to throw you out of the hive. Write a paragraph to explain why you are not like other bees and why you should be allowed to remain in the hive—even though you don't do your share of the work. Be convincing.

_____
_____
_____
_____
_____
_____
_____
_____
_____
_____
_____
_____

© 2000 J. Weston Walch, Publisher   88   10-Minute Poetry Activities Across the Curriculum

Days

Some days my thoughts are just cocoons—
all cold, and dull, and blind,
They hang from dripping branches in the grey
woods of my mind;

And other days they drift and shine—such free
and flying things!
I find the gold-dust in my hair, left by their
brushing wings.

—*Karle Wilson Baker*

> TEACHER PAGE

Days

Procedure

Read the poem out loud to your students and ask them to listen to the images without worrying about what they mean. After a couple of readings, ask students to select the images that seem the most powerful to them. Write these on the board and briefly discuss them. Do they describe what it feels like to have a bad day or a good day? Show an overhead of the poem and ask students to read the poem with you. Then, have students work together with a "poetry partner" to memorize the poem.

Activity Sheet A is a word search puzzle featuring words relevant to Karle Wilson Baker's life. Activity Sheet B has students identify the states where Baker lived and taught, and the places of publication of several magazines that published her work.

Interdisciplinary Activities

1. **Literary map and time line** Karle Wilson Baker was born in Little Rock, Arkansas, in 1878. Notice the "e" added to Karl in an attempt to make the name more feminine. She attended public schools and later the University of Chicago, where she studied with the poet William Vaughn Moody. When Baker was 19, the family moved to Nacogdoches, Texas. She taught high school and did some free-lance writing before marrying Thomas Ellis Baker in 1907. She died in Nacogdoches in 1960. She is considered an outstanding Texas writer of the twentieth century. Have students add Baker to the classroom map and time line. (Language Arts, Social Studies)

"When I Am Blue" list After students become familiar with the poem, ask that each write a "Things to Do When I Am Blue" list. To get them started, write a few suggestions on the board:

> When I am blue, I talk to a friend.
> When I am blue, I go for a long walk.
> When I am blue, I eat chocolate.

These thoughts can be turned into a "Blue Poem." Take this opportunity to discuss how to handle the bad days we all have. (Language Arts, Writing)

2. **Poem illustration** Ask students to draw or paint a picture that illustrates this poem. (Art)

3. **Mime** Have a group of students develop a pantomime to accompany the reading of this poem. (Language Arts)

4. **Poetry reading** Distribute poetry anthologies to groups of students. Ask that each group find at least three other poems that express moods such as happiness, sadness, loneliness, etc. Students should copy the poems onto separate sheets of paper and illustrate them if they wish. These poems will be posted on the bulletin board after a class poetry reading. Allow some time over a couple of class periods for this work. If possible, have students meet in the library on the day of the poetry reading. If not, rearrange the seats in a circle or in some other fashion to distinguish the classroom from its ordinary look. Have one group read one poem, and then ask another group to read a poem expressing the same feelings. Continue in this fashion until all the poems have been read. The situation should be relaxed enough that students feel free to discuss a poem after it is read. (Language Arts)

Answers

Activity Sheet A

Texas: Where Baker lived most of her life after the age of 19
Chicago: Where Baker attended college
Alamo: Site of famous Texas battle
Frost: A poet and friend
Lowell: Amy Lowell, an acquaintance
Nocogdoches: Where Baker's family moved when she was 19
Vaughn Moody: Baker's teacher at the University of Chicago

Other words in the puzzle include:

poet	acme
be	mean
ark	troop
low	hot
wag	able
swag	lend
well	bad
rose	

Activity Sheet B

1. *Little Rock*: Arkansas
   University of Chicago: Illinois
   Nacogdoches: Texas
   Bristol: Virginia
   Columbia University: New York
   Berkeley: California
   Stephen F. Austin State Teachers College: Texas

2. *Yale Review*: New Haven, Connecticut (still published)
   Scribner's Magazine: New York City (no longer published)
   Atlantic Monthly: Boston (still published)
   Century Magazine: New York City (still published under the name *Harper's Magazine*)

Activity Sheet A

STUDENT PAGE

Name _____ Date _____

Days: Word Search

In this word search, you will find a number of words that refer to some part of Karle Wilson Baker's life or to her adopted state. These are listed below. In addition, you will find many other everyday words. How many additional words can you identify? Add these words to the list. As a final challenge, identify the significance of each word listed below; write your answers on the back of this sheet.

```
N V C H I C A G O
A A D P O E T T O
C U F R O S T B E
O G A R K A R L E
G H E L O W E L L
D N D O A S W A G
O M A A C M E A N
C O S D T R O O P
H O T E X A S D E
E D A B L E N D N
S Y R B A D O O S
```

Texas
Chicago
Alamo
Frost
Lowell
Nacogdoches
Vaughn Moody

Additional Words:

_____
_____
_____
_____
_____
_____
_____
_____
_____

© 2000 J. Weston Walch, Publisher   92   10-Minute Poetry Activities Across the Curriculum

Activity Sheet B

STUDENT PAGE

Name _____ Date _____

Days

1. Karle Wilson Baker lived, attended school, and taught in a number of locations. What are the names of the states that can claim a connection to this poet? Schools she attended and in which she taught, as well as the locations of her homes, are listed below. Find the states in which these cities and schools are located.

   Little Rock _____

   University of Chicago _____

   Nacogdoches _____

   Bristol _____

   Columbia University _____

   Berkeley _____

   Stephen F. Austin State Teachers College _____

2. Karle Wilson Baker's work was published in the magazines listed below. Where are (or were) these magazines published?

   Yale Review _____

   Scribner's Magazine _____

   Atlantic Monthly _____

   Century Magazine _____

   Place a check mark next to those magazines that are still published.

© 2000 J. Weston Walch, Publisher   93   10-Minute Poetry Activities Across the Curriculum

The Plaint of the Camel

Canary-birds feed on sugar and seed,
    Parrots have crackers to crunch;
And as for the poodles, they tell me the noodles
    Have chickens and cream for their lunch.
        But there's never a question
        About *my* digestion—
      Anything does for me!

Cats, you're aware, can repose in a chair,
    Chickens can roost upon rails:
Puppies are able to sleep in a stable,
    And oysters can slumber in pails.
        But no one supposes
        A poor Camel dozes—
      Any place does for me!

Lambs are enclosed where it's never exposed,
    Coops are constructed for hens;
Kittens are treated to houses well heated,
    And pigs are protected by pens.
        But a Camel comes handy
        Wherever it's sandy—
      Anywhere does for me!

People would laugh if you rode a giraffe,
    Or mounted the back of an ox;
It's nobody's habit to ride on a rabbit,
    Or try to bestraddle a fox.
        But as for a Camel, he's
        Ridden by families—
      Any load does for me!

A snake is as round as a hole in the ground,
    And weasels are wavy and sleek;
And no alligator could ever be straighter
    Than lizards that live in a creek,
        But a Camel's all lumpy
        And bumpy and humpy—
      Any shape does for me.

—*Charles Edward Carryl*

TEACHER PAGE

The Plaint of the Camel

Procedure

Begin by reading "The Plaint of the Camel" aloud to your students.

Show the poem on an overhead and ask the class to repeat it with you. Because of its length, assign your students no more than a stanza or two a day to memorize. Allow them ample time to work with their poetry partners on memorizing the poem.

Activity Sheet A asks students to research the camel's eating habits, then develop a menu for a camel restaurant. Activity Sheet B asks them to create a comic strip to illustrate the poem.

Interdisciplinary Activities

1. **Literary map and time line** Charles E. Carryl was born in New York City in 1841. He attended private schools and chose business as his profession. Although this poem suggests a fun-loving attitude toward life, Charles Carryl selected a rather humorless career: He was a stockbroker on Wall Street. He wrote one serious book, *The Stock Exchange Primer,* but the majority of his work was similar to "The Plaint of the Camel." The lesson your students can learn from this information is that there may be much more to a person than what is seen on the surface.

    Carryl and his wife had two children, Guy and Constance, and he wrote much of his work for his children. He died in 1920. Add Carryl's name to the classroom time line and note his birth place on the literary map. (Geography, Language Arts)

2. **Choral reading** Groups of students might enjoy rehearsing and presenting a choral reading of this poem for children in the lower grades. The artists in the room could draw and paint props depicting the various animals mentioned in the poem. (Art, Speaking)

3. **Poem parody** This poem is easily parodied. Your students might compose "The Lament of a Teenager." To get them started, write the following lines on the board:

    > Parents dine on steak and wine,
    >   Babies have soft foods to sup
    > And as for the pets, we are told by the vets
    >   Fine meats are cut up for the pup.
    >   But there's never a question
    >   About my digestion—
    >   Anything does for me!

    With this start, they should be off and writing. (Language Arts)

4. **Researching camels** Ask students to research the subject of camels. Both the Internet and reference books will supply a great deal of information about these "ships of the desert." To guide their work, have them start with the following questions, and then add any other interesting information they discover.

    1. Where are camels found?
    2. What foods do they eat?
    3. Camels have the reputation of having difficult dispositions. Is this true?
    4. Why is the camel able to exist in the heat and dryness of the desert?
    5. What is the purpose of the camel's hump?
    6. How large is the camel?
    7. What does the camel contribute to the lives of the desert people?

    The class will benefit if oral reports are given on this subject. (Technology, Science)

Activity Sheet A

STUDENT PAGE

Name _____ Date _____

The Plaint of the Camel

The camel described in Carryl's poem needs a good meal. Actually, he and his friends deserve a good walk-in restaurant. Develop a menu for a camel restaurant. Research the camel's eating habits; then let your imagination wander.

1. Begin by cutting out the menu model below. Fold it on the dotted lines.

2. Decide on your restaurant's name.

3. Finally, list the foods that will be offered and the prices. Don't forget to decorate and add color to the menu.

Activity Sheet B

STUDENT PAGE

Name _____ Date _____

The Plaint of the Camel

There is a good deal of humor in Carryl's poem. Create a five-frame comic strip, one for each of the stanzas, based on what you think best illustrates its meaning. Below each frame, write the line of the poem the frame illustrates. For example, you might illustrate the first frame by showing canaries feeding on sugar and seed. When you have finished, cut out your comic strip and tape it to a piece of plain paper. You may exhibit it on the classroom walls or place it in your portfolio. Use the space below or a separate sheet of paper.

Name _____ Date _____

Our Lips and Ears

If you your lips would keep from slips,
    Five things observe with care:
Of whom you speak, to whom you speak,
    And how and when and where.

If you your ears would save from jeers,
    These things keep meekly hid:
Myself and I, and mine and my,
    And how I do and did.

—*Unknown*

Our Lips and Ears

Procedure

This is in many ways a mystery poem because there is no trace of the person who wrote it. Read "Our Lips and Ears" to your class and then show it on an overhead. All students should be able to appreciate its message. Ask them to sum up the poem's advice in a sentence or two. Discuss the old game of Gossip. If your students have never played it, demonstrate how dangerous gossip can be by whispering a message to one of your students and having that student whisper the message to the next student and so on. When the message has gone around the room, ask the last person to repeat it aloud. Write both that and what you said to the first student on the board, and compare the two messages. This game demonstrates that we don't always hear what was said, and that gossip can easily grow and change. Its potential to hurt others should be underlined.

Activity Sheet A asks students to interview WWII veterans. Activity Sheet B also calls for an interview, this time of anyone who remembers World War II.

Interdisciplinary Activities

1. **Imaginary biography** Since the author of "Our Lips and Ears" is unknown, ask your students to write an imaginary biography of this mystery poet. Students should consider whether the poet is male or female and whether the poet comes from some region of the United States or perhaps from Canada or England. They should also give the poet a name, birth date, education, family, etc. They might even describe the poet's other poems, or such personal details as favorite foods. Ask each student or each student group to write a final copy of this biography to read aloud to the class. If you wish, the class could have a contest to select the biographies they find funniest, most convincing, most unbelievable, etc. (Language Arts, Social Studies, Geography)

2. **Poster** Ask students to draw a poster to illustrate "Our Lips and Ears." Write the poem below the picture. (Art)

3. **Paragraph** Have students write a paragraph conjecturing as to how this poem lost its author. The paragraph should be written from the poem's point of view. (Language Arts)

4. **Literary map and time line** Ask students to decide how "Unknown" should be identified on the classroom map and time line.

5. **Who and whom** This poem offers a good opportunity to review the use of "who" and "whom." Discuss the third line of the first stanza. Point out that "whom" does no action. In this case, it follows a preposition, although it may also be the object of a verb. "Who," on the other hand, *does* something; it is the subject of a verb. Offer the following sentences as examples:

   (a) To whom did you speak?
       ("You" is the subject of the verb.)
   (b) Who will speak?
       ("Who" is the subject of the verb.)
   (c) Who called?
       ("Who" is the subject of the verb.)
   (d) It doesn't matter whom you called.
       ("You" is the subject of the verb.)

   (Language Arts)

Activity Sheet A — STUDENT PAGE

Name _____ Date _____

Our Lips and Ears

During World War II, "Loose lips sink ships" was a popular phrase. The fear of enemy spies was so great that signs with this phrase were posted throughout the United States. Men and women in the armed forces were told what kinds of information they should include in their letters home. They were given a list of subjects to leave out. For example, they were warned against talking about their location, transportation facilities, and military forecasts. To ensure that everyone was careful, each letter home was read and censored. This may seem unbelievable in a country in which free speech is a constitutional right. However, the government rescinded some rights during the war out of fear.

In this activity, you will encourage people who lived through World War II to loosen their lips. You want them to tell you what they remember about the war. Your first step is to create a list of questions to ask. Before you can do that, you need to do some research. Listed below are some topics that relate to World War II. Find out the relevance of each by using the Internet or any book about the war. After you have the information, write out your questions on the the back of this page. Then conduct your interviews.

1. air-raid sirens
2. air-raid wardens
3. ration stamps
4. scrap metal
5. blackout curtains
6. Franklin Delano Roosevelt
7. paper drives
8. war bonds
9. food
10. gas rationing

© 2000 J. Weston Walch, Publisher   100   10-Minute Poetry Activities Across the Curriculum

Activity Sheet B   **STUDENT PAGE**

Name _____ Date _____

Our Lips and Ears: Interview Sheet

The United States declared war on Japan on December 7, 1941, after the Japanese attacked Pearl Harbor in Hawaii. U.S. soldiers also joined in the fight against Hitler in Europe. Thus, the U.S. was involved in war in two different parts of the world.

Try to interview someone who remembers World War II. Anyone who was six years old or older at this time will probably have memories of the war. You may find that you will only need to refer to your questions occasionally once the interview starts. Just mentioning key words will probably encourage most people to talk. Try words like *food rationing, war bonds, paper drives,* and *blackouts.* You might start by saying, "What was food rationing like?"

List your questions below. If you run out of room on the front, use the back of this sheet for your answers.

1. _____
   _____
2. _____
   _____
3. _____
   _____
4. _____
   _____
5. _____
   _____

© 2000 J. Weston Walch, Publisher   10-Minute Poetry Activities Across the Curriculum

Concord Hymn

By the rude bridge that arched the flood,
    Their flag to April's breeze unfurled,
Here once the embattled farmers stood,
    And fired the shot heard round the world,

The foe long since in silence slept;
    Alike the Conqueror silent sleeps;
And Time the ruined bridge has swept
    Down the dark stream which seaward creeps.

On this green bank, by this soft stream,
    We set to-day a votive stone,
That memory may their deed redeem,
    When, like our sires, our sons are gone.

Spirit, who made those heroes dare
    To die, and leave their children free,
Bid Time and Nature gently spare
    The shaft we raise to them and thee.

—Ralph Waldo Emerson

TEACHER PAGE

Concord Hymn

Procedure

If you have already worked with "The Mountain and the Squirrel," the class will be familiar with Emerson's name. Remind them that he is a nineteenth-century writer, and thus many of his words are unfamiliar. This poem is best enjoyed as a choral reading. Read it aloud once, and then show the poem on an overhead. Divide the class into three groups. Each group should read a stanza, and then everyone should read the fourth stanza together. After the poem has been read once, ask each group to discuss where pauses are necessary for effect. Then, stage another reading.

Activity Sheet A has students define words from the poem that may be unfamiliar. Activity Sheet B asks students to compare and contrast "Concord Hymn" and the first stanza of "Paul Revere's Ride."

Interdisciplinary Activities

1. **The Revolutionary War** Ask the class what war is being discussed in this poem. Most should recognize the reference to the Revolutionary War. Mention that the monument described in the poem was erected in memory of the Battle of Concord, which was fought on April 19, 1775. If possible, have students read a description of the events leading up to the war in their social studies books. In addition, suggest that some might enjoy reading Esther Forbes's *Johnny Tremain*, which relates the events of that crucial time period in American history from the point of view of a young boy. A summary of the book might spark interest in it. (Language Arts, Social Studies)

2. **Concord, Massachusetts** Have students use Internet resources to discover more about Concord, Massachusetts. Many famous literary figures lived in Concord, including Louisa May Alcott, the author of *Little Women*. (Technology, Language Arts)

3. **War poems** Two other poems in this book can be linked to "Concord Hymn." Discuss the "Hymn" as it relates to "The Dark Hills" by E. A. Robinson and "In Flanders Fields" by John McCrae. Questions to get discussion going might include:

   1. What is the attitude of each poet toward war?
   2. What might be the reason for the differences in attitude?

   (Social Studies, Language Arts)

4. **"The Shot Heard Round the World"** Organize a class assembly or a school assembly on April 19 to commemorate the "shot heard round the world." For a school assembly, ask each class to sing a song, recite a poem, or prepare an interesting fact sheet about that famous day in American history. Your class can do a choral reading of "Concord Hymn." (Music, Social Studies, Speaking)

5. **Revolutionaries in your area** If you live in one of the original colonies, find out how many men from your area served in the Revolutionary War. Check with your local historical society. If they are not helpful, organize a visit to a local cemetery, where students can actually check for gravestones of Revolutionary War veterans. If you can do this around Memorial Day, the graves will be marked with small American flags. (Social Studies)

Activity Sheet A

Student Page

Name _____ Date _____

Concord Hymn

Your first step in completing this assignment is to write a definition for each of the following words. Use context clues to help you decide on the meaning. When you have finished, check in the dictionary to see if your definitions are accurate. Remember, all languages change. Some words fall out of use. Some are added. The meanings of others change over time.

1. rude _____
_____

2. unfurled _____
_____

3. embattled _____
_____

4. slept _____
_____

5. votive _____
_____

6. redeem _____
_____

7. shaft _____
_____

8. sires _____
_____

9. hymn _____
_____

10. soft _____
_____

Activity Sheet B   STUDENT PAGE

Name _____ Date _____

Concord Hymn

Locate Boston and Concord, Massachusetts, on your map. Legend has it that Paul Revere, a Boston silversmith, rode between Boston and Concord on the night of April 18, 1775, to warn people that the British were coming. You will remember from your study of American history that, up until that time, this country was a colony of England. In 1775, more and more people were upset with the laws that England imposed. Revolution was in the air. Read the following lines from a poem written by Henry Wordsworth Longfellow. He gives his interpretation of April 18, the day before the battle.

PAUL REVERE'S RIDE

Listen, my children, and you shall hear

Of the midnight ride of Paul Revere,

On the eighteenth of April, in Seventy-five;

Hardly a man is now alive

Who remembers that famous day and year.

—Henry Wadsworth Longfellow

(continued)

© 2000 J. Weston Walch, Publisher   105   10-Minute Poetry Activities Across the Curriculum

Activity Sheet B (continued)

STUDENT PAGE

Name _____ Date _____

Concord Hymn

1. What similarities do you see between this stanza and the first stanza of "Concord Hymn?" _____
   _____
   _____

2. In what way is the mood of "Paul Revere's Ride" different from "Concord Hymn"?
   _____
   _____

3. Later in the poem, it is said that Revere rode from Charlestown to Concord to warn the people that the British were coming. How many miles is it from Charlestown to Concord?
   _____
   _____

4. Why do you think Longfellow addressed the readers as "my children" in the first line of the stanza? _____
   _____
   _____

5. The entire poem does not accurately describe the ride to warn of the approach of British soldiers. Research the events of April 18, 1775. Then read the entire poem. How does Longfellow's poem differ from actual events?
   _____
   _____
   _____
   _____

© 2000 J. Weston Walch, Publisher   106   10-Minute Poetry Activities Across the Curriculum

Thanksgiving Day

Over the river, and through the wood,
   To grandfather's house we go;
     The horse knows the way,
      To carry the sleigh,
  Through the white and drifted snow.

Over the river, and through the wood,
   Oh, how the wind does blow!
     It stings the toes,
      And bites the nose,
  As over the ground we go.

Over the river, and through the wood,
   With a clear blue winter sky,
     The dogs do bark,
      And children hark,
  As we go jingling by.

Over the river, and through the wood,
   Trot fast, my dapple grey!
     Spring over the ground,
      Like a hunting hound,
  For 't is Thanksgiving Day!

Over the river and through the wood—
   And straight through the barn-yard gate;
     We seem to go
      Extremely slow,
  It is so hard to wait.

Over the river, and through the wood—
   Now grandmother's cap I spy
     Hurra for the fun!
      Is the pudding done?
  Hurra for the pumpkin pie!

—Lydia Maria Child

TEACHER PAGE

Thanksgiving Day

Procedure

Lydia Maria Child was born on February 11, 1802, in Medford, Massachusetts. At a time when the only place for a woman of her class was the home, Child was active on a number of fronts. She was an ardent abolitionist who, along with her husband, joined in anti-slavery activities. She was also a writer of novels, poems, and political material. She wrote the first American cookbook, *The Frugal Housewife,* and founded the first monthly magazine for children, *Juvenile Miscellany.* Few today know of her many accomplishments. If she is remembered, it is for "Thanksgiving Day," which she entitled "The New-England Boy's Song About Thanksgiving Day."

Begin work on this poem by asking how many know "The New-England Boy's Song About Thanksgiving Day." Probably no one will recognize the poem by that title. Next, ask if anyone knows a Thanksgiving poem. Someone will probably repeat at least the first stanza of the poem. Continue by reading the poem aloud, asking students to join in when the stanzas are familiar. If many are familiar with the poem, have "poetry partners" team up to practice the stanzas.

Activity Sheet A provides a frame for students to write their own updated version of "Thanksgiving Day." Activity Sheet B asks students to create a restaurant's Thanksgiving dinner menu.

Interdisciplinary Activities

1. **Literary map and time line** Add Lydia Maria Child to the classroom time line and the literary map. Ask students to identify other poets that they have learned about who lived at the same time as Lydia Child. Ask them to guess what other author she might have known, given that poet's birthplace. (Language Arts, Social Studies, Math)

2. **Musical accompaniment** Ask the music teacher to find the music that was written to accompany this poem. If possible, learn the name of the person who wrote the music. Your students will enjoy being able to sing the words of the poem. Music will also make it easier for them to memorize the poem. (Music)

3. **Title variations** In addition to "Thanksgiving Day" and "The New England Boy's Song About Thanksgiving Day," "Over the River and through the Wood" is often used as the title of this poem. Ask students to check poetry anthologies and the Internet to discover which title is most often used. At the same time, students can look for additional verses to share with the class. It might be interesting to compare several versions of the poem. Have students hypothesize as to why the changes were made and why some verses are more popular than others. (Language Arts, Technology)

4. **Currier and Ives** The lithographers Currier and Ives documented this period of American life in a series of prints showing ordinary people in everyday pursuits. If possible, find copies of some of their prints. Like Child's poem, they make life in the nineteenth century seem cozy and comfortable. (Currier and Ives prints are frequently used on Christmas cards.) Discuss the reality of wood-burning stoves, candle-light, horse-drawn carts, etc., with your class. It might be interesting to have students look at a Currier and Ives print to identify all the changes that have taken place since the nineteenth century and then depict the same scene in this century. Another question to ponder is what the next century might bring. Assign an essay on this subject. (Art, Language Arts, Social Studies)

5. **Poem illustration** Have students illustrate each stanza of the poem. Display these illustrations on a bulletin board along with key phrases from the poem. (Art)

Activity Sheet A   **STUDENT PAGE**

Name _____   Date _____

Thanksgiving Day

Write a contemporary version of "Thanksgiving Day." A frame for your poem is given below. Cross out any unneeded words. You will need a title.

_____
                              TITLE

Over the _____ and through _____,

To _____ we go;

_____ knows the way,

To _____ the _____,

Through _____.

Over the _____ and through _____,

Oh, how _____ !

It _____,

And _____,

As over _____.

Now reread your work and make any changes needed. Write a clean copy of your poem. Illustrate the page if you wish.

Activity Sheet B   STUDENT PAGE

Name _____ Date _____

Thanksgiving Day

You are the manager of a restaurant planning a Thanksgiving dinner for your patrons. What will you serve? You may decide you want a menu that reflects a particular part of the country or of the world. Will you serve traditional Thanksgiving fare? Or will you feature specialties from your great-grandmother's kitchen? You must offer at least three choices under each section of the menu. Include a descriptive phrase to entice your customers. For example, don't say "mashed potatoes," but rather, "potatoes combined with cream and butter and mashed to perfection."

Appetizers: _____

_____

_____

Soups: _____

_____

_____

Side dishes: _____

_____

_____

Entrees: _____

_____

_____

Desserts: _____

_____

_____

Waltzing Matilda

Once a jolly swagman camped by a billabong,
Under the shade of a coolibah tree,
And he sang as he watched and waited till his billy boiled,
"Who'll come a-waltzing Matilda with me."

Chorus:
    Waltzing Matilda, waltzing Matilda,
    Who'll come a-waltzing Matilda with me;
    And he sang as he watched and waited till his billy boiled,
    Who'll come a-waltzing Matilda with me.

Down came a jumbuck to drink at that billabong,
Up jumped the swagman and grabbed him with glee;
And he sang as he shoved that jumbuck in his tucker bag,
"You'll come a-waltzing Matilda with me."

Chorus:

Up rode the squatter, mounted on his thoroughbred,
Down came the troopers, one, two, three;
"Whose is that jumbuck you've got in your tucker bag?"
You'll come a-waltzing Matilda with me.

Chorus:

Up jumped the swagman and sprang into the billabong,
"You'll never catch me alive," said he;
And his ghost may be heard as you pass by that billabong,
You'll come a-waltzing Matilda with me.

—A. B. "Banjo" Paterson

Teacher Page

Waltzing Matilda

Procedure

Read "Waltzing Matilda" aloud to your class and then show it on an overhead. Divide the class into groups and ask each group to read a stanza with everyone chiming in on the last line: "You'll come a-waltzing..." If you wish, the chorus can be repeated after each stanza, which will be most effective if everyone reads it together. Ask students to read through the poem, drawing a line under every unfamiliar word. When they are finished, have them find a synonym or a definition for each underlined word.

Activity Sheet A guides students to find the meanings of unfamiliar words, and to tell the "story" of the poem using the meanings they find. Activity Sheet B is a scrambled word puzzle of words that refer to either A. B. "Banjo" Paterson or to "Waltzing Matilda."

Interdisciplinary Activities

1. **Song versions** Although A. B. "Banjo" Paterson wrote the original version of this song, variations of the song were also written by Harry Nathan and Marie Corvan. The version on the student page is the version most commonly sung today, but it is not the same as the version Paterson originally wrote. Have students research to find the history of this song, which nearly became the Australian National Anthem. (Language Arts, Social Studies, Music)

2. **Literary map and time line** A. B. "Banjo" Paterson was born in 1864 in Narambla, New South Wales. He died in 1941. He lived a very colorful life, which your students will enjoy researching on the Internet. At various times, he was a journalist, lawyer, jockey, farmer, soldier, and poet. It might be interesting to post some of his poems on a classroom bulletin board, as they have the flavor of Australian English. Add his name and birth date to the class time line and literary map. (Language Arts, Social Studies, Technology)

3. **The settling of Australia** Ask one group of students to research the settling of Australia. Separated groups might explore who settled this continent, when, and why, the unusual animals of Australia, the geography of the region, and the plants of Australia. (Language Arts)

4. **Music to "Waltzing Matilda"** Ask the music teacher to teach your class the melody for "Waltzing Matilda." (Music)

5. **Distance to Australia** Have students use a world map to calculate the distance between Australia and your school. (Math)

Answers

Activity Sheet A

billabong—waterhole
billy—tin with wire handle used to boil water, heat food
coolibah—type of eucalyptus tree
jumbuck—sheep
matilda—bedroll
squatter—landowner
swagman—unemployed drifter
trooper—policeman
tucker—food
waltz—walk along a bush track

Story: A drifter camped by a waterhole in the shade of a eucalyptus tree. As he waited for water to boil in a tin, he sang about walking through the bush carrying a bedroll. When a sheep came to drink at the waterhole, the drifter grabbed it and put it in his food bag. Soon after, the landowner came up with several policemen and asked him about the sheet. Rather than let himself be arrested for theft, the drifter jumped into the waterhole, and drowned.

Activity Sheet B

1. jumbuck
2. swagman
3. Australia
4. ghost
5. tucker bag
6. Narambla
7. coolibah
8. lawyer
9. Banjo
10. Paterson
11. billabong

Activity Sheet A

STUDENT PAGE

Name _____ Date _____

Waltzing Matilda

Some of the words in "Waltzing Matilda" are slang words. Some are words that have a specific meaning in Australia, where this song was written. Using books and the Internet, find the meaning of each of these words. Write the meaning beside each word.

billabong _____

billy _____

coolibah _____

jumbuck _____

matilda _____

squatter _____

swagman _____

trooper _____

tucker _____

waltz _____

Now, on the back of this sheet or on a separate piece of paper, write out the story of "Waltzing Matilda" in your own words.

Activity Sheet B

STUDENT PAGE

Name _____ Date _____

Waltzing Matilda

All the following scrambled words refer either to A. B. "Banjo" Paterson's life or to "Waltzing Matilda." Can you figure out all eleven?

1. UKBMJUC _____
2. MGSAAWN _____
3. LAATRIUSA _____
4. THSGO _____
5. KTREGA UCB _____
6. MAABALRN _____
7. HCLIBOOA _____
8. RWYLEA _____
9. NABOJ _____
10. RESAOTPN _____
11. BOINLGALB _____

Write a sentence about A. B. "Banjo" Paterson using scrambled words. See how quickly your classmates can decipher your sentence.

_____
_____
_____
_____

© 2000 J. Weston Walch, Publisher   114   10-Minute Poetry Activities Across the Curriculum

We Real Cool

The Pool Players

Seven at the Golden Shovel.

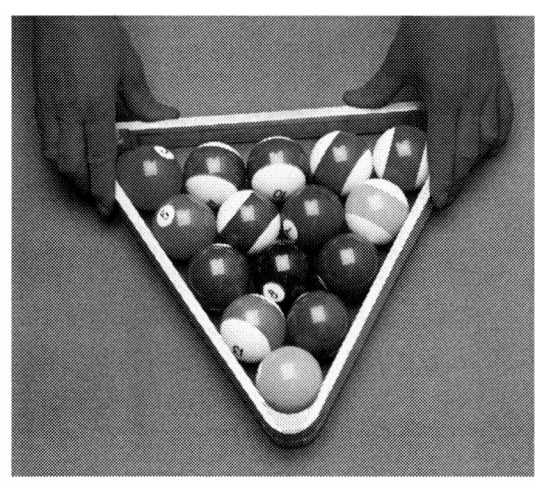

We real cool. We

Left school. We

Lurk late. We

Strike straight. We

Sing sin. We

Thin Gin. We

Jazz June. We

Die soon.

—Gwendolyn Brooks

TEACHER PAGE

We Real Cool

Procedure

"We Real Cool" is a poem that should be introduced to the class by members of the class. Early in the week that you intend to introduce this poem, ask seven of your students to meet with you to discuss it. Distribute copies of the poem and ask each person to read one line, with everyone joining in on the last line. Timing is everything with this poem, so have students practice it a couple times before the poem is presented to the class. Student interest in the poem should be high by the time this group has finished their presentation. Give the class a few minutes to memorize the poem before asking volunteers to interpret the poem.

In discussing the poem, be sure to point out the full title of the poem and to comment that a golden shovel is often used to bury things. Ask why Brooks has used "street" language. To make the point, have students write the poem as a narrative. They should recognize that the playful combination of street language and rhythm is akin to the raps of today.

Activity Sheet A directs students to find out information about Ms. Brooks, then present it in an interview format. Activity Sheet B has students create masks as a preparation for Interdisciplinary Activity 3.

Interdisciplinary Activities

1. **Literary map and time line** Gwendolyn Brooks was born on June 17, 1917, in Topeka, Kansas. Her family moved to Chicago, which remains her home today. Brooks has received many awards; she was the first African-American writer to be appointed to the American Academy of Arts and Letters and to win the Pulitzer Prize. Ask a student to research the Pulitzer Prize and report back to the class. As an ongoing assignment, have students find out how many of the poets that they have studied were recipients of the Pulitzer Prize. Add Brooks to the literary time line and map. (Language Arts, Social Studies, Geography)

2. **What is cool?** Have students create a "Cool Sheet." Write the words "Cool is:" on the board or on an overhead. Have students offer examples of what they consider cool. Discuss what "coolness" is. Share with them some of the things that were cool when you were in school. Suggest that coolness changes quickly and is not a true aspect of a person. (Language Arts)

3. **Making masks** Have students draw a mask. Students can use paper bags, material affixed to sticks, or any other approach they can think of. When the project is finished, ask students to wear their masks during a class. Conduct the class as usual. At the end of class, ask students if wearing masks changed the way they reacted to the lesson. You might want to distribute a survey asking about the masks before any discussion takes place. Connect this activity with "We Real Cool" by asking what kinds of masks the "cool" people in the poem were wearing? (Language Arts, Art)

4. **Writing alternative poems** Have students write their own versions of "We Real Cool." Any one of the following lines should help your reluctant writers get started:

    We real wild

    We real happy

    We real late

    We real bright

    (Language Arts, Writing)

5. **Objects in Brooks's poetry** To motivate students to further investigate Brooks's poetry, bring a large glass container into the classroom. Explain that each week you will place in the container an object about which Brooks has written a poem. Begin with a can of beans, which is linked to "The Bean Eaters." Lead them to "Narcissa" by placing a pair of jacks in the container. After a few weeks have students choose their own objects to represent her poems. (Language Arts, Social Studies)

Activity Sheet A

STUDENT PAGE

Name _____ Date _____

We Real Cool

In her poetry, Gwendolyn Brooks deals with everyday subjects and people. She is very much a poet of the people. If you were able to interview her, what would you would like to ask her? List the questions below. Then do the research necessary to answer them. Write up your findings as an interview. You will find an example below:

Question: "Ms. Brooks, where do you get the ideas for your poems?"

Answer: "I get most of my ideas from my own experience. I have been an observer of people my whole life."

Question: _____

Answer: _____

_____

Question: _____

Answer: _____

_____

Question: _____

Answer: _____

_____

Question: _____

Answer: _____

_____

Activity Sheet B

STUDENT PAGE

Name _____ Date _____

We Real Cool

Below are examples of masks from around the world. Using them for inspiration, draw your own mask on a piece of construction paper or a paper bag. You may use whatever materials you have available, for example, markers, paint, pencils, crayons, fabric, glitter, etc. Don't forget to cut holes for the eyes and mouth. If you use construction paper, cut your mask out and glue or tape it to a stick. You can then hold it up to your face. If you use a paper bag, you can simply put the bag over your head.

African   Inuit   African

Greek   Indonesian   Native American

© 2000 J. Weston Walch, Publisher   118   10-Minute Poetry Activities Across the Curriculum

Eldorado

    Gaily bedight,
    A gallant knight,
In sunshine and in shadow,
    Had journeyed long,
    Singing a song,
In search of Eldorado.

    But he grew old—
    This knight so bold—
And o'er his heart a shadow
    Fell as he found
    No spot of ground
That looked like Eldorado.

    And, as his strength
    Failed him at length,
He met a pilgrim shadow:
    "Shadow," said he,
    "Where can it be—
This land of Eldorado?"

    "Over the Mountains
    Of the Moon,
Down the Valley of the Shadow,
    Ride, boldly ride,"
    The shade replied,—
"If you seek for Eldorado."

—*Edgar Allan Poe*

TEACHER PAGE

Eldorado

Procedure

To lend an air of mystery to the first reading of this poem, darken the room and ask students to remain very still as you read. Read the poem slowly and dramatize the word "Eldorado." When you have finished, ask students what they think "Eldorado" represents. Draw a web on the board consisting of a circle with spokes reaching out from the center. On the spokes write the words the class supplies. Accept all possibilities before explaining that "Eldorado" is a mythical city of fabulous wealth and thus represents happiness to some people.

Activity Sheet A gives students a brief biography of Poe, then asks them to support statements about Poe based on information in the biography. Activity Sheet B guides students to explore the poem, then relate it to their own lives.

Interdisciplinary Activities

1. **Literary map and time line** After students have finished Activity Sheet A, have students search the Internet for further information on Edgar Allan Poe. There should be plenty of interest in this activity, as students will be intrigued by the fact that so much of this poet's life and death remains a mystery. Ask for a written report that can be read to the class. Add Poe's name to the literary map and the class time line. (Language Arts, Social Studies)

2. **Short stories on video** Rent a video of one of Poe's short stories. "The Cask of Amontillado" has mystery and a surprise ending. "The Tell-Tale Heart" is also a good choice, as is "The Mask of the Red Death." (Language Arts)

3. **Poem recital: "The Raven"** "The Raven" is one of Poe's best known poems. Ask a small group to recite the poem. Students may want to develop props to accompany their presentation. (Language Arts)

4. **Attaining the unattainable** The poem may well leave students confused as to why the knight never reaches "Eldorado." Discuss the difficulty in attaining any ideal. If one is always looking for something better, it is difficult to appreciate the present. (Language Arts)

5. **Connections to Don Quixote** Your students may be interested to learn about a literary character Poe's knight resembles. In 1605, Miguel de Cervantes wrote of Don Quixote, a gentlemen who addles his brain by reading too many chivalric novels about knights righting the wrongs of the world. Quixote sets forth on his quest, battling windmills he thinks are giants, sheep he thinks are armies, and a student he mistakes for the Knight of the White Moon. He, like Poe's knight, cannot accept and enjoy reality. An encyclopedia will furnish more information, and you should be able to find drawings of Don Quixote and his faithful friend, Sancho Panza. In addition, ask students to look up the word "quixotic" in the dictionary, where they will find that this literary character gave the world a new word. (Language Arts)

Activity Sheet A

STUDENT PAGE

Name _____ Date _____

Eldorado

Read the brief biographical sketch below. Then answer the questions that follow.

> Edgar Allan Poe was born in Boston, Massachusetts, in 1809. He died in Baltimore, Maryland in 1849. Poe's parents were actors who died before he was three. John Allan of Richmond, Virginia, took the young orphan into his home. Poe was educated for five years in England. He then returned to the United States to enter the University of Virginia.
>
> He enjoyed gambling, and this got him into trouble with John Allan. Allan refused to pay off Poe's debts. He forced Poe to break off his engagement to Sarah Elmira Royster, his childhood sweetheart. Poe entered the army and later, with Allan's help, enrolled in West Point. This, too, turned into a disaster, and he was dismissed. Allan gave up on Poe, who went to live with his Aunt Maria Clemn and her daughter, Virginia. Throughout this period, Poe wrote. He turned to this profession to support himself and what would soon be his new family.
>
> Poe fell in love with 14-year-old Virginia Clemn, and the two were married in 1835. At the same time, he became editor of the *Southern Literary Messenger*. Poe had already published *Tamerlane, Al Aaraaf, MS Found in a Bottle,* and *The Narrative of Arthur Gordon Pym*. It seemed that success was imminent. Unfortunately, Poe began to drink heavily. In 1837 Poe lost his job because of his drinking.
>
> His pursuit of literary recognition took him to New York City and Philadelphia. During this period, Poe wrote "The Fall of the House of Usher."

(continued)

Activity Sheet A (continued) **STUDENT PAGE**

Name _____ Date _____

Eldorado

Virginia died in 1847. Poe was devastated, as can be seen in his semi-autobiographical poem "Annabel Lee." His own death in 1849 is shrouded in mystery. He was on a lecture tour at the time. Shortly before his death, he was reunited with his childhood sweetheart, Sarah Elmira Royster, and the two planned to marry. He left her in Richmond while he traveled to New York. There he intended to inform Virginia's mother, Mrs. Clemn, of his engagement. No one is sure why he went to Baltimore, where he was found unconscious in the street, and later died. He may have been mugged, succumbed to some disease, or collapsed in an alcoholic stupor. There is evidence to support each theory. Unfortunately, theories are all that we have. This man who invented the detective story left his readers with one final mystery.

Support the following statements with information from this brief biography of Poe's life and death.

1. Poe's childhood was unsettled.
    1. _____
    2. _____
2. Poe's behavior could sometimes be described as reckless.
    1. _____
    2. _____
    3. _____
3. Poe was a prolific writer.
    1. _____
    2. _____
    3. _____
4. Poe's death remains a mystery.
    1. _____
    2. _____

Activity Sheet B

STUDENT PAGE

Name _____ Date _____

Eldorado

Refer to Poe's poem to answer the following questions.

1. What is the knight's mood as he begins his journey? _____
   _____

2. Produce evidence to support your answer to question 1. _____
   _____

3. Why does he become discouraged in the second stanza? _____
   _____

4. Support your answer to question 3. _____
   _____

5. What is meant by the words "pilgrim shadow"? (Refer to a dictionary for help.) _____

6. Does the pilgrim encourage or discourage the knight? _____
   _____

7. Support your answer to question 6. _____
   _____

8. Do you think the knight will ever reach Eldorado? Why? _____
   _____
   _____

9. How would you describe the Eldorado you are searching for? _____
   _____
   _____

10. If you had been the shadow, what advice would you have given the knight? _____
    _____

Share Your Bright Ideas with Us!

We want to hear from you! Your valuable comments and suggestions will help us meet your current and future classroom needs.

Your name_____Date_____

School name_____Phone_____

School address_____

Grade level taught_____Subject area(s) taught_____Average class size_____

Where did you purchase this publication?_____

Was your salesperson knowledgeable about this product?   Yes_____   No_____

What monies were used to purchase this product?

___School supplemental budget   ___Federal/state funding   ___Personal

Please "grade" this Walch publication according to the following criteria:

Quality of service you received when purchasing .... A   B   C   D   F
Ease of use .... A   B   C   D   F
Quality of content .... A   B   C   D   F
Page layout .... A   B   C   D   F
Organization of material .... A   B   C   D   F
Suitability for grade level .... A   B   C   D   F
Instructional value .... A   B   C   D   F

COMMENTS:_____
_____

What specific supplemental materials would help you meet your current—or future—instructional needs?
_____

Have you used other Walch publications? If so, which ones?_____

May we use your comments in upcoming communications?   ___Yes   ___No

Please **FAX** this completed form to **207-772-3105**, or mail it to:

Product Development, J. Weston Walch, Publisher, P.O. Box 658, Portland, ME 04104-0658

We will send you a **FREE GIFT** as our way of thanking you for your feedback.   **THANK YOU!**